Spiritual Exercises
For Today

Spiritual Exercises
For Today

A CONTEMPORARY PRESENTATION
OF THE CLASSIC SPIRITUAL
EXERCISES OF IGNATIUS LOYOLA

Tad Dunne

HarperSanFrancisco
A Division of HarperCollins*Publishers*

FIRST EDITION

Library of Congress Cataloging-in-Publication Data

Dunne, Tad, 1938–
    Spiritual exercises for today : a contemporary presentation of the classic Spiritual exercises of Ignatius Loyola / Tad Dunne.
    —1st ed.
      p.   cm.
    ISBN 0-06-062108-7 (alk. paper)
    1. Spiritual exercises. 2. Ignatius, of Loyola, Saint, 1491–1556. Exercitia spiritualia. I. Ignatius, of Loyola, Saint. 1491–1556. Exercitia spiritualia. II. Title.
BX2182.2.D85   1991
248.3—dc20   90-55344
                                                CIP

91 92 93 94 95 MART 10 9 8 7 6 5 4 3 2 1

To Dorothy and Otto

Contents

Acknowledgments   *xi*

Introduction   *xiii*
Observations for the Retreatant   *1*
Observations for the Mentor   *8*

PART 1: THE FOUR WEEKS   *13*

First Week   *13*
God Will Act   *15*
The Purpose of Life   *17*
A Reign of Praise, Justice, and Peace   *18*
The Good News   *20*
Repentance   *23*
Sacrament of Reconciliation   *39*
Recognizing Christ   *41*

Second Week   *43*
The Spirit of Christ   *45*
Discipleship   *48*
Structure of the Exercises   *51*
Passages from the Hidden Life of Christ   *55*
Pull and Counterpull   *59*
Passages from the Public Life of Christ   *68*

Third Week   *79*
The Spirit of Compassion   *81*

The Law of the Cross   *85*
Structure of the Exercises   *88*
Scriptural Passages   *92*

Fourth Week   *97*
The Spirit of Forgiveness   *99*
Structure of the Exercises   *102*
Scriptural Passages   *105*

PART II: OTHER EXERCISES   *111*

Contemplations to Experience Love   *113*
You Must Love the Lord   *115*
You Must Love Your Neighbor   *119*

Examination of Consciousness   *122*
Neurosis   *124*
Class Consciousness   *125*
Story Line   *126*
Sins of Omission   *127*

Spiritual Exercises for Healing   *128*
Facing the Hurt with Christ   *132*
Facing the Person Who Hurt You   *133*
Facing Your Compromises   *134*
Facing Yourself   *135*
Facing the Future   *137*

Prayer of Remembering   *138*

Praying the Psalms   *141*

A Prayer to Christ Our Model
by Pedro Arrupe, S.J.   *144*

PART III: SPIRITUAL GUIDELINES *147*

Revelation *149*

Making a Decision *151*
Three Kinds of Discipleship *151*
Three Types of Deliberation *152*
Directives *153*

Dynamics of Spirit *161*
Spiritual Consolations and Desolations *161*
The Angel of Light *167*

Dynamics of Story *170*

Notes *176*

Acknowledgments

I would like to express my gratitude to a number of people who have contributed valuable suggestions on earlier drafts, in particular to Bill Barry, S.J., Dick Baumann, S.J., Fred Benda, S.J., Sal Briffa, S.J., Moira Carley, and Carla Mae Streeter, O.P. I also want to thank the members of the Boston College Lonergan Seminar for their contributions as I was writing a final draft: Pat Byrne, Joe Flanagan, S.J., Philip Fleuri, Fred Lawrence, Matt Lamb, Tim Lynch, Sebastian Moore, O.S.B., Al Nudas, S.J., and Louis Roy, O.P., as well as to the participants at the "Loyola & Lonergan Workshop" (Boston College, March 17–18, 1989) who contributed excellent directives on the texts "Purpose of Life" and "Dynamics of Story."

Special thanks go to those who supported me with their companionship and care, in particular to Howard Gray, S.J., to the members of the Barat House Jesuit Community, to Tom Ewens, and to the Jesuit novices at Loyola House, Berkley, MI, during the years (1983–88) I struggled to provide spiritual mentoring that was theologically sound, and to two people who years ago welcomed me into their family, and to whom this work is dedicated: Otto and Dorothy Seebaldt.

Introduction

The spiritual exercises suggested in this manual are designed to enable you to make or to deepen a commitment with your life. Although there might be some profit in working through the manual alone, it will be far more effective if you use it with the help of a mentor or a companion who also has a copy.

The sequence of exercises is modeled after the *Spiritual Exercises* of Ignatius of Loyola (1491–1556), a short manual with a profound and enduring effect on Christian spirituality. It is a classic, and yet it is in need of some adaptation in view of developments in philosophy, historical criticism, trinitarian theology, and Scriptural studies.

Specifically, you will find the following adaptations:

- Ignatius' "First Principle and Foundation" is revised to be more in line with the Jewish Shema and the two great commandments of Christ.

- During the First Week, exercises on healing of memories and emotions have been added. This addition seems particularly important in today's wounded societies.

- The work of the Holy Spirit is presented in balance with the work of Christ Jesus.

- There is a stress on contemplating the reality of God's action on our behalf, rather than merely exercising intellect, emotions, and imagination for their own sakes.

- "Grace" is considered not as a general state of one's soul but more empirically as an occurrence in consciousness. You will ask to experience very specific graces during the exercises.

- Ignatius' "Two Standards" parable is offered as a model of a theology of history. You are invited to develop a personal theology of history along similar lines.

- "Rules for the Discernment of Story" have been added to complement Ignatius' "Rules for Discernment of Spirits." This will help you discern the myths that originate either from your own subconscious or from society.

- The graces of the Third and Fourth Weeks are more explicitly focused on "Jerusalem" as representing the world God cares for. It is the focus for both the agony and the joy of Jesus' Spirit.

- Ignatius' "Contemplation to Experience Love for God" has been complemented by a "Contemplation to Experience Love for Neighbor."

The justification for the adaptations I have made can be found in the companion to this volume, *Spiritual Mentoring: Guiding People through Spiritual Exercises to Life Decisions*. That volume discusses the fundamental dynamics of spirituality as well as fundamental doctrines about God and the Kingdom relevant to a retreat.

The exercises are divided into four "Weeks." Each Week corresponds not to a seven-day period but to a distinct kind of inner experience. So the exercises may be made over the period of a year, or several months, making one exercise per day. Part of it may be made more intensely; for example, retreating into solitude for a week and making four or five exercises a day.[1]

The four Weeks are not steps to take and leave behind. Rather, they build toward a cumulative engagement with the full, divine dimensions of human history. The first two Weeks build toward a commitment, a concrete decision to direct your life along a path motivated by the living God. The last two Weeks deepen your share in the compassion of God for the world and in the assurances God brings to the world through you. By the end you can expect to have an abiding sense of sin and grace in history (First and Second

Weeks) and a shared sorrow and joy with God (Third and Fourth Weeks).

Normally, you would progress from the beginning to the end, because the graces of each Week build on what went before. But within any Week there may be some benefit in skipping ahead or returning to some exercise. As a criterion for which exercises to do, ask yourself, What will better dispose me now to receive from God the experience I desire during this Week?

Observations for the Retreatant

1. The purpose of these exercises is to dispose you to experience the understanding, energy, and courage to make a major decision in your life. The decision may be about changing jobs, getting married, moving, having children, volunteering in some charitable enterprise. Or it may be about withdrawing from unethical practices in business or speaking up against them. The change may be a matter of putting your present way of living more explicitly into the hands of God. Indeed, a change of attitude can be much more revolutionary than a change of circumstances.

2. A "spiritual exercise" is very much like a physical exercise—it is meant to tone up your spiritual sensibilities to the point where you quickly recognize and respond to movements of God in your life. It is also a "school of prayer" because you learn how to move to prayer quickly and to recognize traps in prayer more easily.

Some of these exercises will be difficult, just as some physical exercises are difficult. But that does not mean they "didn't work" or that you "failed." In fact, the effort spent working in an exercise that seems dry helps to strengthen your determination. Normally an exercise lasts between twenty minutes and an hour.

3. It is very important to begin the exercises with as much generosity as possible. This means being generous with your time and being faithful to the work of the exercises. More important, it means being generous with what you are will-

ing to give up for the sake of letting God direct your life. Imagine yourself without this person, that habit, these skills, those possessions, and relying on God to direct your every choice. Imagine preferring the consolations that God alone can give to the securities and comforts that surround you. It means being generous in driving out compulsive preoccupations from your mind and energetically fighting any thought that draws you away from God.

4. You may discover that after the First Week you do not feel drawn toward making a major decision, or that something is holding you back. It will be wise either to postpone continuing the retreat until you do reach some clarity or to enter the Second Week asking God to give you that clarity. Keep in mind, however, that a decision to deepen your familiarity with God while keeping your present commitments is no small achievement. It will require a commitment to prayer and sharing your faith with others in a way that will make you a different person before very long.

The Third and Fourth Weeks are exercises in realizing how Christ walks with you in your decision. So, if after the Second Week there is still no clarity, it will not help to continue the retreat. In this case you might consider whether or not there is some psychological healing needed before you can make a responsible choice about the future.

5. You will often ask for a "grace." This is not some abstract status you enter in God's eyes. Grace is an inner experience; it is something that occurs in your consciousness. You are asking to experience a desire, or an insight, a realization, a conviction, or some feeling during the exercise itself.

For example: to feel a confirmation of a choice you have made; to feel Jesus' own sorrow as he weeps over Jerusalem; to deepen your realization that God gives you your life at the present moment; to recognize and appreciate the Spirit as Love at work in your heart; to acknowledge your deepest fears. During the various Weeks of the exercises, these graces you ask for will vary, depending on the subject matter.

Name the experience you want and seek it out. God resides in you as Infinite Spirit; beg God to move in you.

These "graces" during the exercises are needed to help you with the central grace you are asking for: the wisdom to recognize where God is calling you, and the love and desire to act.

6. Try as much as possible to stay in the truth. During a retreat it is easy to get lost in your imagination, your concepts, or your feelings without any reference to something real. To stay in the truth requires a desire to know the truth—about human history, about God, and about yourself. Set yourself the goal of facing the full truth no matter what. Come with the desire never to fool yourself about who you are, who God is, what history is.

To know the truth about yourself means being ready to connect the various exercises to the data of your own life. You will bring your own concerns, whatever they may be, into the prayer to talk about them with God. It means bringing all your limitations and sins as well.

To know the truth about God means more than a mere notional assent to truths taught in the Christian tradition. It means coming to know something about God that is directly connected to your own experience. It is not a matter of understanding some complex explanation but of savoring some reality. Still, real assents to divine truths normally begin from familiarity with Christian doctrines on the revealed truths. So it will also help to review the dogmatic presuppositions listed in the section "Revelation" (p. 149) every once in a while to keep afresh what God has revealed.

To know the truth about human history means stepping outside of yourself and seeing the entire stream of human life as a single, flowing reality. This not only gives an objectivity about yourself in the larger scheme of things but more easily draws you into cooperating with the work of God in the world.

Realizing and relishing one truth will have a far more powerful effect on you than making a thousand rational, analytical connections.

7. All of the exercises are designed to help you realize and relish the truth. Although the exercises aim toward living in the truth, they do not approach the truth through theological understanding. Rather, they lead through the "three eyes of love"—your imagination, your affectivity, and your realizations. These reveal paths to take far more clearly than logic and analysis.

As you begin each exercise, imagine the real situation you intend to pray over, being especially aware of any feelings you want to experience. When you use your imagination or affectivity, however, do not lose connection with the reality. If you are "thinking about yourself," use your imagination to see God in the picture; God, after all, is certainly present. If you have certain feelings about yourself, imagine God's intimate presence. These feelings in the presence of someone who loves you are far more reliable than feelings about yourself that occur when you imagine you are alone.

In meditating on ideas, particularly on the texts of Paul, ask yourself, I may understand this, but do I *know* it? For example, Paul says that our baptism is a burial with Christ (Rom 6:1–11). A notional assent to this idea is easy. A real assent means realizing that your own "deaths"—experiences of loss you can recall—are an essential part of your baptism.

If you are imagining scenes taken from the Bible, give credence to the effect the drama has on you, even though you may know very well that the scene was a construction by some biblical author. The author's purpose—an inspired purpose—was not to give an accurate historical report but to draw you into a scene affectively.

8. Begin each exercise by asking God to help you keep your focus. Ask for the grace that during the exercise everything you think of doing, all your external bodily motions, and all interior experiences may be consciously directed toward responding to and sharing in God's work.

9. During the exercise, do not focus on yourself without reference to God. Focus first on what God has been doing. Come with a strong desire to learn about God, to feel a desire to be drawn by God, and to act in obedience to the graces God gives.

Then reflect on yourself, what you have been thinking about during the day, what you have been hoping for, what disappointments you have been suffering.

10. During the exercise, or at least at the end, talk directly to Jesus (or Mary or the disciples) in these scenes as one friend talks to another. Or talk directly to the Father. Let your imagination allow their side of the conversation to arise naturally, rather than trying to think of what they might say. These spiritual conversations with God are absolutely vital.

Be conscious that in these dialogs you are moved by God's own Spirit. Your most intimate union with God as Spirit is to cooperate with the movements of love for the Father and Son that the Spirit gives.

If the dialog seems stilted or artificial, or if the conversation brings any kind of spiritual desolation, then withdraw from it, putting your trust in the Spirit. "When we cannot find words in order to pray properly, the Spirit himself expresses our pleas in a way that could never be put into words. And God, who knows everything in our hearts, knows perfectly well what he means, and that the pleas of the saints expressed by the Spirit are according to the mind of God" (Rom 8:26–27).

11. Whether you begin with Scripture or with your personal experience, it is important to connect the two. For exam-

ple, you may begin with Scripture. In Mt 4:23 you might read about "painful complaints" or about "people who lived in darkness." Connect these to your life experiences: What "painful complaints" have you been making recently? What "darkness" do you live in? Or, in the parable of the sower, what part of your life is the path's edge, the rock, the thorns? Or in the parable of the prodigal son, what do the five gifts that the father gives represent in your life?

Or you may begin from your life. Often the poignancy of your present situation prevents you from doing otherwise. You will probably need a Bible concordance to find the passages in Scripture that resonate with your experience. But as you pick a representative word, it is often more fruitful to use as your cue a feeling rather than an idea. For example, you may feel some anxiety about a trip you have to make. The idea of "trip" might suggest the Book of Tobit or Mary's trip to visit Elizabeth. But the feeling of anxiety suggests perhaps Martha's anxiety about cooking or, at Cana, Mary's anxiety about wine. Jesus' response to their anxieties will often be more helpful to you than your own reflections about what a trip entails.

12. If your prayer is dry, if you find it difficult or artificial to say things directly to God or to Jesus in the scene, consider what you ought to be able to say. Or reflect on what a person on retreat would likely say at this point. Or imagine yourself teaching someone else in such a way that you arouse deep desire in them. In any case, work your imagination to speak the words you want to feel.

If you are frequently distracted by practical obligations, keep a pen and paper handy to jot down reminders and set them aside. Anytime you become distracted, rather than return to the point you last remember, it is better to make a strenuous effort to recall the experience you asked for in this exercise. Reenter the exercise by begging for this grace.

Be careful to use a posture that helps you get what you want. What posture would be appropriate if you already experienced the grace you ask for?

Close the exercise with a short formal prayer or psalm that seems suitable. See "Praying the Psalms" (p. 141) for help in choosing something appropriate.

13. After each exercise, follow up with a short examination of what happened: What graces did God give? Did you get the grace you asked for? What temptations did you experience? How well did you respond? Is God leading you somewhere or warning you in any way?

When you meet your mentor or companion, you do not have to describe how each exercise went. Instead, bring the results of your examination of the exercise, which will be more an assessment of what happened to you rather than a narrative of what you did. Bring to light any questions or doubts you have, whether they occurred during the exercise or not, no matter how slight they may seem.

Observations for the Mentor

1. It is important to let God work with the retreatant's inner experiences directly, no matter how dull or unusual they may seem to you. Your work is to bring the person to articulate his or her desires and to help discern which experiences are really from God.

2. When the retreatants meet with you, do not elaborate on insights or emotions that fascinate you. Pay closer attention to whether these movements draw them toward God's work or away from it, remembering that even the devil can quote Scripture and use the truth. The amount of credence you give to their insights or feelings depends not on the objective worth of the things they think or feel; it depends rather on how clearly these insights or feelings originate from their love of God and neighbor. See "Dynamics of Spirit" and "Dynamics of Story" (pp. 161, 170) for guidelines here.

While talking with them, if they have been seeking joy in God, do not respond to moods of sadness; if they have been seeking sorrow in God, resist joy. Keep very clearly in mind the grace they asked to experience in each prayer period. Sometimes it will be given, and sometimes the evil spirit gives anxiety or an experience that fakes the genuine grace they seek.

3. It is very important that retreatants do not consider either the good inspirations or the evil temptations as originating from themselves. On the one side lies presumption; on the other lies despair.

For this reason it is helpful for many retreatants to talk about the pulls of grace and the counterpulls from grace as the work of good and evil spirits. What individuals do with those pulls, of course, becomes their own work and their own responsibility. Choice alone should be cause for any subsequent gratitude or shame, not the mere experience of inclinations, no matter how strong.

4. Watch that retreatants stay in reality. Insights need verification, data, validation. Emotions should respond to realizations about how things truly stand; they should move toward commitment, decision, and action. Imagination should be exercised to help realize what actually happened historically or what actually happens in the person's own soul.

5. Be attentive to whether the retreatant is addressing the Father, or Jesus, or the Spirit as "you" or "he" or "she." It may be natural for a while to think of God in the third person, but this should move to a personal, face-to-face address, with the conviction of faith that God is truly and immediately present.

Be attentive also to whether the retreatant in fact is aware of the role of God's Spirit in the heart and God's Word in our history, both as God's gifts of the divine self. In any religious experience whatsoever, all three Persons come to us, whether or not we recognize it, but it helps greatly to welcome the true, trinitarian God explicitly, and with proper understanding of the difference between the visible, historical mission of God as Word and the invisible, interior mission of God as Spirit.

6. Retreatants should not describe everything that happened in their prayer. This can convey the impression that you hold them accountable to you. Rather, they should bring the fruits of their examination of prayer—whether God moved them or not; what graces were given; what temptations were experienced; what questions they have about their experiences. In short, more understanding than

description, although some descriptions will certainly be necessary.

7. It can be very helpful to repeat exercises. Although there are many suggestions given in this manual, in no way should they all be done. It is much better to return to an exercise that the retreatant feels drawn to repeat—sometimes because the first time was rewarding and sometimes because it was not. If you suggest a specific repetition, be careful not to give the impression that there is more in the text yet to dig out. Follow their intuition about which repetition seems to draw them.

If you feel at a loss about what to suggest for prayer, ask what grace they want to experience especially this Week of the retreat. Use a concordance, if necessary, to find Scripture passages that resonate with this experience. This can help them claim the desire as their own, rather than expect the exercises to work some change outside their own freedom.

8. Be attentive to whether the purpose of each Week is clear to the retreatant. And be prepared to suggest ending after the First or Second Week if he or she is not disposed to make a major decision or deepen a commitment already being lived out.

Thus, the First Week helps dispose a person to see the reality of sin in the world, including personal sin, and to welcome God's tender mercies. It is a great grace to realize that we cannot keep from sin by our own power. We may wish to, but we are powerless to move our own wills without the gift of willingness from God. It helps to provide some ritual closure to this Week, either by a confession of sin or some other liturgical rite of God's forgiveness.

The Second Week aims at deepening and making concrete a person's desire to do something for the world God so loves. The meditation on "Pull and Counterpull" is a very important vision of what every person in the world is fundamentally about. If a retreatant has some alternative ideology about the human struggle, it is extremely important that he or she destroy it and replace it with at least some consistent vision of world process from God's point of view. In some cases this "metanoia"—a change of mind, a change of one's imaginal theology of history—can be crucial enough to constitute a major decision. It represents a conversion on the psychic level, in which a new image of world process becomes the backdrop for all further decisions.

Ritual closure is likewise important for the end of this Week; a renewal of baptismal vows, as a sign of readiness to die and rise with Christ, would be fitting.

The Third Week aims at deepening a person's sense of union with God, particularly through the mystery of suffering and death. It fosters an awareness of walking in God's Agonizing Spirit and in the company of Christ and of all suffering humanity. Be watchful that the retreatant not slip back into an attitude of trying to "reach" God, through prayer or good works. It takes an act of faith to believe that God has already "reached" us in Christ and the Spirit. An appropriate ritual closure to the Third Week would be the Eucharist, particularly as it symbolizes the paschal mystery.

The Fourth Week, similarly, aims at deepening a person's awareness of this concrete unity with God, but particularly as walking in a peaceful and confident hope. It is a profound grace to feel joy precisely because Jesus is joyful and that God's purposes are being realized. A ritual closure to the Fourth Week would be a simple, happy meal together, in the spirit of the meal at the seashore in John's Gospel, as the retreatant walks forward in the Spirit of the living Christ.

PART I

The Four Weeks

First Week

*"Repent! The Reign of God
is at hand!"*

God Will Act

These passages are meant to instill great desires and hope for what God will accomplish in the days to come. Meditate on them in any way you see fit, for no fixed time period. Add passages of your own in the space provided at the end of each list of scriptural texts.

1. Isaiah 55. "Come to the water, all you thirsty. . . . With you I will make an everlasting covenant. . . . As the rain waters the earth, so my word will not return to me empty." God's very tender and very effective love.

2. Hos 11:1–9. "When Israel was a child I loved him. . . . I was the one looking after them. . . . I led them with reins of kindness . . . like someone who lifts an infant close against his cheek."

3. Is 43:1–7. "I have called you by name, and you are mine. . . . You are precious in my eyes . . . and I love you. . . . Do not be afraid, for I am with you."

4. Lk 12:22–31. "Do not worry about your life. . . . Think of the flowers: they neither spin nor weave, yet even Solomon . . ."

5. Psalm 139. "Lord, you search me and know me. . . . Where could I go to escape your spirit?"

6. Psalm 63. "You are my God, . . . my soul is thirsting for you. . . . I long to gaze on you in some sanctuary . . . for you have always helped me."

7. 1 Sm 3:1–19. Call of Samuel: "'Speak, Lord, your servant is listening.' . . . Samuel grew up and the Lord was with him and let no word of his fall to the ground."

8. Jn 3:22–36. John the Baptist: "'The joy I feel is now complete. . . . He must grow greater, I must grow smaller.' . . . Anyone who believes in the Son has eternal life."

9. Gn 22:1–18. Sacrifice of Isaac: "You have not refused me your son, your only son."

The Purpose of Life

This is a set of considerations to ponder about why God has put us on this earth. It is meant as an orientation to the entire retreat. Read it over and consider what it means for several days.

We are created to love the Lord our God with our whole hearts, with our whole souls, with our whole minds, and with all our strengths, and to love our neighbor as ourselves. God created the entire universe as a good place for us to exercise this love creatively.

Unhappily, because of our self-centered love, we have so impoverished our world that no place can be found that fosters love as it might. And we have so impoverished ourselves that we have both a weak will and a corresponding lack of perception of spiritual reality. Therefore, we do not easily know what is most conducive to loving God and neighbor.

Yet in Jesus God has personally entered this chaos, turning our attention to where the divine gaze is fixed: on the victims, the marginalized, the crucified. And in the Spirit God personally enters each of our hearts to recognize the work and example of Jesus in our history, and to heal our creativity that has been wounded by sin.

So now, through the work of Jesus and the Spirit, our one desire and choice can be whatever is more conducive to loving God all the way and loving our neighbors as ourselves.

A Reign of Praise, Justice, and Peace

Here are some Scripture passages on the original order and harmony God intended for creation. As you pray over these, ask for grace to understand the true meaning of "justice" and of "peace." Ask for an intimate and abiding perception of the fact that God desires to direct human history in a way that creates genuine community among all people. Ask also to experience God's own desires as your own.

1. Gn 1:1–2:4. Creation. God's own Spirit hovers over an original chaos. At God's word each thing is created. God's creation has man and woman at its center, made in God's own image and likeness.

2. Wis 11:21–27. "In your sight the whole world is like a grain of dust that does not tip the scales. . . . Yet you love all that exists, holding nothing of what you have made in abhorrence. . . . You spare all things because all things are yours, Lord, lover of life—you whose imperishable Spirit is in all."

3. Psalm 104. The glories of creation. "Lord, how great you are! . . . You stretch the heavens out like a tent. . . . You fixed the earth on its foundations. . . . You made the moon to tell the seasons, the sun knows when to set. . . . All creatures depend on you. . . . You stop their breath, they die; You give breath, fresh life begins. . . . I mean to sing to the Lord all my life!"

4. Psalm 105. The Lord's faithfulness to his people; the history of Israel. "Yes, faithful to the sacred promise given to his servant Abraham, the Lord led his happy people forward, to joyful shouts from his chosen."

5. Psalm 136. Litany of thanksgiving—for nature and for Israel's history. "He made the great lights—his love is everlasting. He led his people through the wilderness—his love is everlasting."

6. Psalm 139. "Lord, you search me and know me; you know when I sit and when I stand." How close God is to me.

The Good News

Now listen to the good news as announced by Jesus. The texts below describe the fundamental attitudes that ought to show in anyone who hears Christ. Hear it with a keen awareness of your own anxieties and fears. Especially if you consider yourself a deeply committed follower of Christ, return again to the original message in all its simplicity.

THE MESSAGE OF JESUS

Ask for the grace to experience a deep sense of welcome and joy to the reassurances given by God. Or ask for an understanding of Christian life-style that will become second nature to you.

1. Mt 5:1–16 (Lk 6:20–26). The Beatitudes. Before reading this text, imagine yourself feeling at home in the company of those listening to Jesus. Recall the ways in which you are destitute ("poor in spirit"), lowly, mourning, longing for justice, merciful, pure in heart, a peacemaker, and persecuted.

2. Mt 5:13–48 and Lk 12:1–12. The gospel and the law. Again, in solidarity with people oppressed by officials, recall your own frustrations over the hypocrisies of any "scribes and Pharisees" in your life.

3. Lk 6:27–38 (Mt 5:43–48). The new standard of compassion.

4. Lk 6:39–49 (Mt 7:1–5, 21–27). Self-responsibility.

5. Lk 12:22–34 (Mt 6:25–34). Trust in God.

6. Mt 6:1–24. Examples of true righteousness.

7. Lk 11:1–13. On asking God for what you need.

WHO IS MY NEIGHBOR?

Ask for the grace to feel genuine solidarity with the entire human family, but particularly the poor and oppressed whom Jesus favored. To experience the impoverishment of spirit you share with ordinary people, you might make some exercises in a bus station.

1. Lk 10:29–37. The Good Samaritan. Call to mind the disenfranchised and beaten in today's society. Be as concrete as you can. What kind of people does the priest and the Levite in you want to pass by on the other side of the road?

2. Mt 25:31–46. The Last Judgment. "I was hungry and you gave me food." Consider that Jesus is not disguised as hungry in order to test our generosity to the poor. Jesus is eternally in solidarity with anyone hungry. His love favors those who hunger. The God you seek is all around you.

3. Jas 2:1–9. Looking down on the poor. "'Stand over there.' . . . It was the poor according to the world that God chose, to be rich in faith and heirs to the Kingdom. . . . The supreme law of Scripture: 'Love your neighbor as yourself.'"

Repentance

Here is the grace you are asking to experience during
the exercises that follow: to receive a personal, intimate
understanding of sin and of God's tender mercies—both
in your own life and in the world.

Although you will recall your own specific sins, you are
not asking for the grace to remember them all. You are asking to see what a broken relationship between you and God
really means—how absurd and shameful it is, how destructive it is to all the relationships in your life, particularly to
your relationship with the One who created you in love.

As a help to bringing your past to mind, see "Prayer of
Remembering" (p. 138).

If you have been victimized or wounded in a way that
prevents you from thinking objectively about your own sins,
you may find the exercises under "Healing" helpful (p. 128).

You are also asking for a general understanding of sin
in the world, how since Adam and Eve people have turned
away from God, how the world today is enmeshed in a web
of sin.

It may be appropriate during this Week to symbolize
the death that sin has brought to your life by fasting from
food or from some favorite distraction. It may also be appropriate, at the end of the First Week, to confess your sins to
someone, whether sacramentally or otherwise. For meditating on "sin in the world," it may be enough to read the
morning paper or walk either in a very rich or very poor
part of town.

To help keep your focus you might break up the scriptural material into four distinct points:

1. God's desires for the solidarity of the human family, and how this particular evil violates God's plan.
2. What the effects of this sin are—the evil effects it has on the person's surroundings and the corrupting effect it has on the sinner's own heart and conscience.
3. Who this sinner is—whether yourself, or Israel, your home town, your family—and what arrogance and self-deceit are at work here.
4. What this situation or person would be like if there were no sin. What potential goodness God sees here and longs to bring about.

SOCIAL SIN

These exercises are not directed toward an examination of conscience but rather toward sharing God's own view of sin, seeing the horror of it in community, feeling a mixture of deep repulsion, outrage, and pity.

1. Is 59:1–21. "Your hands are stained with blood, your finger with crime, your lips utter lies. . . . Their plans are sinful plots, violence is their only method. . . . They are quick to shed innocent blood. . . . So justice is removed far away from us and integrity keeps its distance, . . . sincerity is missing and he who avoids evil is robbed."

See the *web* of sin, how our own sins link into the larger sins of society. You may want to use the newspaper for this.

As a mantra, repeat "May your name be held holy."

2. 2 Pt 2:1–22. A meditation of the city. Walk in the decayed part of town for this. "They will eagerly try to buy you, . . . those governed by their corrupt bodily desires and have no respect for authority, . . . self-willed people with no reverence, . . . who only insult anything they do not understand. . . . They will quite certainly destroy themselves. . . . With an infinite capacity for sinning . . . people like this are dried-up rivers, fogs swirling in the wind."

As a mantra, repeat "May your name be held holy."

3. Rom 1:18–32. Paul's description of Corinth—the corruption of a culture and its rationalization by a philosophy.

4. Sin in your family. Call to mind the effects sin has in your family. This may be (a) sibling rivalry; (b) active abuse from parents; (c) passive abuse of neglect; (d) how children repeat the destructive routines of parents. Consider how difficult it is to break out of the routine and beg God to give you the courage and wisdom needed to stop the cycles of sin.

Mantra: "Your Kingdom come!"

5. Ez 18:1–32. The person who sins dies, not his or her parents or children.

The grace to ask for: to recognize personal responsibility for sin, in spite of social and cultural pressures.

Meditative Reading:

Psalm 106. A historical account of how Israel forsook God and how "time and time again God rescued them." A hymn of gratitude for God's fidelity and compassion.

PERSONAL SIN

With these exercises ask not simply to see your sin but particularly to feel true guilt and shame as you face your truth in God's presence. This is the only kind of guilt and shame that is life giving.

1. Gn 3:1–19. "Your eyes will be opened, . . . you will know good and evil. . . . They realized they were naked. . . . 'Where are you?' . . . 'I hid.'"

Consider where you hide from the Lord. Recognize in yourself the essence of sin, the tendency you share with every human being.

The grace: to experience the shame of wrongdoing and the impulse to hide from God.

2. Mt 13:4–23. Parable of the sower.

The grace: to understand the different ways in which the Word does not find root in me, and to feel shame over each way.

Mantra: "Your will be done on earth as in heaven."

3. 2 Sm 12:1–15. Nathan's accusation of David.

The grace: to see a sin I do not wish to see; to let the full truth come out.

Mantra: "Forgive us our sins as we forgive those who sin against us."

4. 1 Jn 1:5–2:2. "If we say we are free of sin, we deceive ourselves, . . . there is no truth in us."

Grace: to deepen the conviction that I am more sinful than I realize and to desire to have it all out before God.

5. Rom 7:13–23. "I cannot understand my own behavior. . . . I fail to carry out the things I want to do and I do the very things I hate. . . . Who will rescue me from this body doomed to death?"

List some of these things—what I wanted to do but didn't; what I hated to do but did.

Grace: to recognize and appreciate how permanently helpless I am to actually do what I choose; to feel a permanent need for the Lord's help at every step of my life.

6. Mt 18:21–35. Parable of unforgiving debtor.

Grace: to see the inconsistency between the forgiveness I want from God and the way I treat others who have wronged me.

Mantra: "Forgive us our sins as we forgive those who sin against us."

7. Mt 25:31–46. The Last Judgment. "I was hungry and you gave me food. . . . Insofar as you did it to the least of my brothers and sisters . . ."

Grace: to be astonished at the number of ways I ignore Christ in my sister or brother.

8. Classic sin: sin of one person, sin of Adam and Eve, sin of pure spirit. These may be taken together or as separate exercises:

a. One person's sin. Imagine a person of your own sex who makes a deliberate choice to live without reference to God. That choice may have been instigated, for instance, by some concrete covetousness or revenge, but it was a deliberate choice nonetheless. Consider how unhappy and enslaved such a person becomes without God's mercy. Consider how that person consistently tears apart the fabric of a community. Then think of how God has not allowed you to be enslaved by very similar choices you have made to live outside of God.

b. The sin of Adam and Eve. The point of this story is to account for the perdurance of sin in the world. Think of how the most ancient sins never really die: their effects are felt on progeny for generations. Or think of the most contemporary sins and how old their roots go, reaching back to a hatred of the light at the beginning of our race. Call to mind the fact that you inherited from your parents many biases and weaknesses, but that there are sins, such as that of Adam and Eve, that were not at all conditioned by parents' attitudes.

c. The sin of the fallen angels. This legend was designed to account for the ultimately spiritual origins of sin, without attributing sin to God. So consider how a personal being, without any encumbrance of bodily passions, would use its own liberty to refuse to reverence God and so is given what it wants. As a pure spirit, it becomes malice itself. Reflect on sins of pure spirit within yourself, conditioned neither by your upbringing nor by your bodily needs.

Ask for the grace to *feel* shame and confusion. Speak with Christ on the Cross, asking three questions: What have I done for Christ? What am I doing for Christ? What, in all justice, ought I to be doing for Christ? The point is to be mortified at realizing how much you ought to do but could not in the face of what Christ chose to do for you.

9. Your own personal history of sin.

The grace: the gift of a growing and intense sorrow, even to the depth of tears. This may be made as a preparation for the sacrament of reconciliation.

10. Personal sins of omission. Recall times when you could have done good for someone else and did not. Recall times when you should have done good to yourself and did not.

Grace: to understand how even though no written law forbids these omissions, they are still sins against God's own Spirit within me. Ask to feel intensely the shame of violating the temple God longs to make of you.

11. Wonder and gratitude.

a. Recall how you share in God's gifts of wit, heart, spirit, beauty, peace, and so on and yet how often you deform them.

b. Realize how all of creation around you and of which you are made supports you in being and cooperates with the laws of nature, and yet you easily bring it all to disharmony by sin.

c. Express heartfelt thanks to God for giving you life this very moment: the air you breathe, your heartbeats, your mind playing with its thoughts, your feelings, your very self.

12. Psalm 38. "No health in my bones because of my sin. ... My guilt is overwhelming me. ... Bowed down, bent double, overcome, I go mourning all the day. ... Yes, I admit my guilt, I am sorry for my sins. ... Lord, do not desert me!"

Grace: to feel deep sorrow and my genuine guilt.
Mantra: "Do not put us to the test!"

13. Meditate your own deathbed. What will you wish you had done with your life? What will be your greatest sadness, your greatest joy? How central a part of your life will you want God to have been?

Grace: the courage to put some sin out of my life from now on.

14. Lk. 15:11–32. The prodigal son.

Watch the son get anxious about his life; leaves home for the excitement of the world; gets disenchanted in his heart; returns humbled, but so human. See the welcome by the father. See each of the five gifts the father gives. Ask to know God more intimately by knowing this Father's own response to sin and harm.

Meditative Reading:

Romans 1–4. An account of how no one has a right to boast about keeping rules. Only faith in God's loving forgiveness gives anyone a right to stand with dignity. What rules or laws have you relied on to give you a sense of worth?

Ezekiel 16. An allegory of how Jerusalem was born a rejected and unloved girl, and how God cared for her, made a promise to her, and made her beautiful. Jerusalem became infatuated with her own beauty and forgot about God, "piling whoring on whoring." But God will be faithful to the promise and forgive her. What have you done with the gifts God has given you since your birth?

Mt 11:17–24. "We played the pipes for you and you wouldn't dance." Reflect on sins of omission. How hateful they are to the loving Christ. What violence they do to the Spirit within. Most important, reflect on how every sin is essentially a sin of omission, that is, not a forbidden action but a refusal to act on the Spirit's inspiration. See also Mt 23:37–39: "How I longed to gather your children as a hen gathers her chicks under her wings, and you refused!"

"LEPERS"

There are a number of situations in which we are rejected and treated as "impure" on account of the color of our skin, our gender, our sexual orientation, a disease, or some addictive behavior. The "lepers" of society. Moral reasoning alone can never give us a sense of dignity in Christ. Even loving acceptance by others will not heal our attitude toward ourselves unless we are able to find "justification" and "righteousness" in an inner faith rather than an external standard. The following exercises address that faith.

1. 2 Cor 12:7–10. Paul was given "a thorn in the flesh" to keep him from becoming proud. Three times he pleaded with God for it to leave him. God's reply was "My grace is enough for you; my power is at its best in weakness."

It is quite doubtful that the "thorn" was a mere physical ailment; Paul would have boasted of his share in Christ's sufferings. More likely the "thorn" was some morally ambiguous attitude or addictive behavior. Paul's faith is shown at the point where he *stops* asking God to remove the thorn and trusts instead that God's power will work through this weakness.

Discernment is needed here to tell when to stop working on a moral difficulty and to trust in God's power. But the lesson for us is that we do not need to make removal of the thorn a condition for our well-being in the Lord. Our well-being is up to God, and God is faithful.

2. Consider that you are made in the image and likeness of God.

Whatever affliction you may have—whether a bodily disease, an addiction, or an outcast status in society—there is no one on the face of the earth without at least some hidden "leprosy."

No one is justified before God, even though many others are able to hide their affliction from the public eye. You are in deep solidarity with them, as made in God's image, as wounded, as called to faith in your dignity and the dignity of others, by the grace of Christ and the gift of God's Spirit.

Speak with Christ in a dialog about your attitude and his attitude toward your affliction. If you find it helpful, write out the dialog as it unfolds. Be aware of the Infinite Spirit of God in both of you, a Spirit that cries "Abba, Father!"

HELL

Life without love of God and neighbor is hell. It will help to contemplate the nature of that hell from Scripture.

1. Lk:15:11–32. The prodigal son (again).

Focus on the elder brother, who is invited to come to the banquet but refuses, clinging to righteousness and resentment as his only pleasure. What a hell this is—to be free to go to the banquet but prefer resentment.

Grace: to realize how I have resisted taking the risk of rejoicing and being happy; to realize what the Father really desires of me. Ask to experience a healthy fear of your own righteousness.

2. Read the texts where Jesus talks about hell.

How anger, being unreconciled with someone, or a lustful thought makes one liable to hell: Mt 5:20–30.

How being a faithful Jew is not enough: Mt 8:5–13; 13:36–43; 22:1–14.

How failure to use what God has given is not tolerated: Mt 25:14–30.

Leading others astray: Mk 9:42–50. Compare Jesus' threats and anger to the way a person whose concerns are ignored by a loved one resorts to stronger tactics.

Grace: to understand how Jesus felt about sin and how he chose these particular metaphors for loss of salvation; to feel his outrage and frustration over sin.

Mantra: "Do not put us to the test. Deliver us from the Evil One."

MERCY

> In these meditations, ask for the grace to experience
> God's mercy, and in particular to understand that God
> is merciful to you not merely for your own sake but
> particularly for the sake of your community.

1. Psalm 51. A petition for new and constant spirit, for joy
and gladness. Recall the sins of omission in your life—the
times you could have risked love but did nothing.

Grace: to lament for my sins of omission; to beg God
the grace of the Spirit of Love in my heart.

2. Rom 8:1–13. How God does for us what the law could not
do: "sent his own Son in a body as physical as any sinful
body" and "gives life to your own mortal bodies through the
Spirit living in you."

Grace: to become deeply familiar with God's life-giving
Spirit living in me.

3. Jn 11:1–44. The raising of Lazarus.

Grace: to feel the loving compassion Jesus has for me
and to feel his power to bring me back to life again and
return me to my family.

4. Eph 2:1–10. "Obeying the spirit at work in the rebellious,
. . . we were living sensual lives, ruled entirely by our own
physical desires and our own ideas. . . . When we were dead,
God brought us to life with Christ. . . . How infinitely rich
he is in grace. . . . We are God's work of art."

Grace: an abiding sense of gratitude.

5. Psalm 103: "Bless the Lord my soul. . . . He redeemed your life from the pit, . . . renewed your youth like the eagle's, . . . is tender and compassionate, slow to anger, most loving. . . . His love lasts for eternity."

6. Romans 6. "When we were baptized in Christ Jesus we were baptized in his death. . . . We are dead to sin, . . . our former selves have been crucified with Christ . . . to free us from the slavery of sin. . . . Make every part of your body into a weapon fighting on the side of God. . . . You are living by grace and not by law."

Grace: to feel released from concern about religious laws and deep desire to live morally through the graces won by Christ.

7. Isaiah 54. "Shout for joy. . . . Do not be afraid. . . . Like a forsaken wife, distressed in spirit, the Lord calls you back. . . . The mountains may depart, the hills be shaken, but my love will never leave you. . . . Remote from oppression, you will have nothing to fear."

8. Jn 15:1–12. The vine and the branches.

Grace: to recognize how being grafted onto Jesus is life, to be cut off is death. To experience his life flowing mercifully through my spirit.

9. Lk 5:1–11. Simon Peter witnesses catch of fish, realizes his sinfulness.

Grace: to imprint on my memory, never to forget, how my sinfulness is revealed only as I recognize Jesus' power.

10. Lk 15:11–32. The lavish father.

Grace: an intimate experience of welcome home by God.

Meditative Reading:

Rom 5:1–11. On the faith necessary to believe (1) God in truth gave the Son up to the death we deserve; (2) God's own Spirit is a gift of love in our hearts, a love we can count on in the face of sufferings.

Romans 6. Our baptism is our pledge of dying with Christ so as to be raised with Christ to live free from any sin that enslaves us.

Ez 36:20–36. God's response to Israel's infidelity: To gather them from abroad, make them prosper, so that other nations will know the holiness of God. "I shall give you a new heart, and put a new spirit in you. I shall remove the heart of stone from your bodies and give you a heart of flesh instead. I shall put my own spirit in you."

Sacrament of Reconciliation

"Confess your sins to one another, and pray for each other, and this will cure you" (Jas 5:16). *Jesus said to his disciples, "For those whose sins you forgive, they are forgiven"* (Jn 20:23).

It is helpful to deal with genuine guilt through confession to another person. God has poured out the Holy Spirit on all believers and enabled each one to forgive you from the heart with God's own forgiveness. As a preparation for such a confession, the following texts may be helpful:

1. Jeremiah 31. "I have loved you with an everlasting love, so I am constant in my affection for you. . . . I build you once more, virgin of Israel. . . . You will go out dancing. . . . They had left in tears, I will comfort them as I lead them back. . . . I will change their mourning into gladness."
   Take this either as addressed to you personally or in its proper historical meaning—how the Lord called Israel back from exile and to this day has been faithful to those who make up the New Israel.

2. Jn 21:1–19. Jesus appears on the seashore.

Notice how every action of Peter has occurred in his life before (fishing, miraculous catch, recognition of Jesus, following Jesus, the questions by the fire) and that now Jesus is recapitulating his life through love and forgiveness. See how Jesus forgives Peter. Feel the atmosphere of the presence of Jesus.

3. 2 Cor 2:14–5:10. A long section on how we are chosen to radiate the Spirit. "Be mirrors reflecting the brightness of the Lord, . . . be earthenware jars holding a treasure, enduring hardships which train us to carry the weight of eternal glory."

4. Hebrews 11 and 12. A long section on the faith of Israel, a "cloud of witnesses on every side of us," on not losing faith in Jesus who endured the cross for us, an encouragement to endure suffering.

Recognizing Christ

After welcoming the good news of the God's Reign from Jesus, and after turning from sin through God's mercy, turn now to Jesus again to gain an intimate understanding of who he is. In this set of exercises you recapitulate the experiences of the first Christians as they slowly realized more about the person of Jesus. These meditations serve as a preparation for the Second Week.

1. Phil 1:21–26; 3:7–16. A meditation on the consolations of life with Christ, "thanks to the help given me by the Spirit of Jesus," sharing in his sufferings and sharing in his glory.

2. Jn 1:1–14. How God's Word was the source of everything created and now comes to earth in person.

3. Rv 21:1–8. "A new heaven and a new earth . . ." Jerusalem dressed as a bride for her husband. "His name will be God-with-them. . . . Every tear will be wiped away. . . . Now I am making all things new. . . . I am the Alpha and the Omega, the beginning and the end."

4. Col 1:15–23. "He is the image of the unseen God, . . . in him were created all things, . . . through him and for him. . . . He holds all things in unity, . . . all things to be reconciled through him and for him."

Second Week

"Come, follow me!"

The Spirit of Christ

Here are two Scripture passages to meditate on. They are about both the dignity and the cost of discipleship with Christ. They are meant as an orientation to the Second Week of the retreat. As you pray over these, ask for the grace to desire to be a partner with Christ in God's Kingdom. Ask to experience this desire in a way that will be effective as you make a concrete choice about some relationship in your life.

2 Cor 2:14–5:10. "Thanks be to God, who makes us, in Christ, partners of his triumph. . . . We are not qualified in ourselves. . . . With our faces unveiled we reflect like mirrors the brightness of the Lord as we are turned into the image that we reflect. . . . We are only earthenware jars that hold this treasure. . . . We are subjected to difficulties on all sides but never cornered. . . . We carry with us in our body the death of Jesus so that the life of Jesus, too, may always be seen in our body. . . . these train us for carrying the weight of eternal glory which is out of all proportion to them. . . . This is the purpose for which God made us, and he has given us the pledge of the Spirit."

Romans 8. "The law of the Spirit of life in Christ Jesus has set you free from the law of sin and death. . . . The Spirit of God has made his home in you. . . . Unless you possessed the Spirit of Christ you would not belong to him. . . . If the Spirit of him who raised Jesus from the dead is living in you, then he will give life to your own mortal bodies through his Spirit living in you. It is the Spirit of heirs, making us cry out, 'Abba, Father!' The Spirit himself and our spirit bear united witness: we are heirs of God and coheirs with Christ, sharing his suffering so as to share his glory. . . . The Spirit comes to help us in our weakness, for when we cannot find words to pray properly, the Spirit himself expresses our plea in a way that could never be put into words. . . . Neither death nor life, no angel, no prince, nothing that exists, nothing still to come, not any power, or height or depth, nor any created thing can ever come between us and the love of God made visible in Christ Jesus our Lord."

Meditative Reading:

These can be done, along with either reading above, anytime during the Second Week to help keep you in touch with your desire to follow Christ and walk in his Spirit.

1 Pt 4:12–5:4. "If you can have some share in the sufferings of Christ, be glad. . . . It is a blessing for you when they insult you for bearing the name of Christ, because it means that you have the Spirit of glory, the Spirit of God resting on you. . . . Even those whom God allows to suffer must trust themselves to the constancy of the Creator and go on doing good. . . . When the chief shepherd appears, you will be given the crown of unfading glory."

Hebrews 11–12. The exemplary faith of Abel, Enoch, Noah, Abraham, Sarah, Isaac, Jacob, Moses, Rahab, and others. "With so many witnesses in a great cloud on every side of us, we too should throw off everything that hinders us, especially sin. . . . Let us not lose sight of Jesus, who leads us in our faith and brings it to perfection. . . . Hold up your limp arms and steady your trembling knees; . . . then the injured limb will not be wrenched, it will grow strong again. . . . We have been given possession of an unshakeable kingdom."

Discipleship

The exercises of the Second Week are designed to help you make some concrete choice about your life within the context of a loving desire to follow Christ.

The first set of exercises focuses on the Incarnation and hidden life of Christ. This is an important background for understanding the value of small beginnings, hiddenness, and waiting for God's Spirit to move.

Next you will find the meditation on the "Pull and Counterpull." This is a crucial meditation because it asks you to consider how all of history is a struggle between two forces that everyone feels in consciousness. Its purpose is to enable you to claim a theology of history appropriate to the needs of your time and place.

There follows a number of passages on the life of Christ, grouped according to theme. Choose among them as the Spirit prompts. In them you should exercise your imagination and feelings rather than your powers of deduction and analysis. This is for the purpose of entering into a real relationship with Jesus as a "you" to talk to, not a "him" to think about.

Take care, however, that your imagination and feelings help you realize the truth of what Jesus did and is doing for you, and to be realistic about your desires to respond. In other words, avoid making a mental film or play out of the scene you contemplate. It may also help to read a biography of a saint or any texts that are likely to stimulate *desire* in you. Avoid texts that stimulate mere *thinking* about Christ.

The purpose of this highly sensate and imaginative approach is to grow in familiarity with your own experiences of desires and fears that originate from the Holy Spirit. By paying attention to the movements within you as you accompany Jesus in his ministry, you will learn to "smell" the difference between a situation in which God is at work and a situation in which God is excluded. Most important, using your imagination and affectivity will help you grow in heartfelt love of Jesus and of his church. Love for Christ is an experience of God's Holy Spirit. This strongly affective love will give you the courage in tougher times to act like a true disciple of Jesus. A woman or man in love makes far better choices than anyone who just calculates and measures.

As you go through the life of Christ, you will consider his own choice to leave his carpentry and his hometown and to begin preaching the Kingdom of God. This may be the best point to begin considering the choices that face you. For this reason you will find the pivotal meditation on the pull and counterpull inserted at the beginning of Christ's public life. The best time to begin, however, is a matter of individual discretion.

What kind of choices should you be considering in your own life? Perhaps it is a change in your state of life—whether to marry or remain single. Perhaps it is a change in the style of your discipleship—whether leaven in the dough where you work or leadership in a Christian community. Or the decision may be about changing how you relate to certain friends, to someone you work with, or to your neighbors. Perhaps you need to confirm a choice you have already made, bringing it before the Lord in prayer. Perhaps you need to consider how well you are living out the situation you are in.

For example, do your everyday choices reflect the same desire for God's Kingdom that first moved you to be a disciple? Do you need to die to some part of your life and let yourself be reborn to another? Do you use the gifts you have with the conscious purpose of bringing about the Kingdom of God?

Whatever the case, be prepared to change some relationship in your life, even if it means undergirding a present relationship with a more explicit love for God. If you do not feel ready to do this, it may be wise to put off continuing the retreat for some time, but be sure to continue asking God for the grace to *want* to be able to change whatever relationship God may be leading you to change.

Plan to make any such decision or confirmation by the end of the Second Week, which, depending on how you are making this retreat, could be anywhere between seven days and seven months. Directives for making a decision can be found in "Making a Decision" (p. 151).

Structure of
the Exercises

There are many ways to use Scripture to exercise the thoughts and feelings that prepare you to make a good decision. The standard way is to read a text as its author meant it to be read. This will entail having some understanding of the author's purpose.

If the passage is a teaching, use your intelligence to reflect on its content, applying it to your situation. In particular, connect the words of the text to your own experiences. For example, in Paul's letter to the Romans, he writes "by faith we are judged righteous and at peace with God" (5:1). What exactly is the experience of being "judged righteous" like? When have you recently felt judged, either by yourself or others, and needed to find a more trustworthy judgment from God? Or if the passage is an obvious directive to, say, "look at the birds of the air; they neither sow nor reap," do look at the birds and discover what trusting in God feels like.

If the passage is a narrative of an event, and particularly if you have been following a set of narratives, use your mind to make a real assent to the fact that these events actually occurred, that these are deeds of God in history, and that the values originating from these events have shaped, in part, the ways in which people act today. Normally a real assent to the deeds of God in history is followed by expressions of gratitude.

There are a number of passages that beg for allegorization, that is, the characters and their development are meant to represent something in the lifetime of the reader. This was a common rabbinic and Hellenic practice. John's Gospel is replete with symbolisms representing universal relationships between any person and God. The synoptic parable of the seed falling on different turfs was probably allegorized even before the composition of the Gospels. In any case, there is a legitimacy to seeing various figures in a vignette as parts of yourself—for example, the Mary versus the Martha in you, or the Nicodemus in you who comes to Jesus only under the cover of darkness. Or the development of an action may represent an event in your own life—for example, how Peter must leave the security of his boat and walk on water, which he can do as long as he keeps his eyes on Jesus. Reflections such as these are not without tradition and merit.

If the passage is a hymn or psalm, use it to express the longing, the praise, the petition, or the gratitude you feel in your heart. It is very helpful to read a psalm aloud. Keep in mind, though, that the psalms were written primarily for a community. So before beginning call to mind real people you know whose good or bad fortune needs to be brought before God. Like a true priest, pray in their stead. For a list of psalm themes, see "Praying the Psalms" (p. 141).

Normally you can either choose a Scripture passage according to some scheme and then see how it applies to your life or, conversely, you can begin from some life experience and look for a passage in Scripture that will help you bring it to God. But during the Second, Third, and Fourth Weeks of the retreat, begin from your life experience of wanting to follow Christ. Then choose from the passages for a given Week as you see fit. The main criterion is what kind of exercise will best dispose you to experience the inner movements you want.

Ignatius Loyola recommended a program of imaginal contemplations of scenes from Christ's life, few of which involved either teaching or miracles, and most of which involved *walking* with him. This restriction stemmed from the

Middle Ages' spirituality of "imitating Christ." See "A Prayer to Christ Our Model" (p. 144) for a prayer by Pedro Arrupe, S.J., which represents this spirituality very well today.

The Ignatian style of contemplation can be very powerful if you allow yourself to become part of the scene, lending a hand, talking to the characters, and letting the scene unfold naturally. It remains an exercise of imagination and emotions, however, and whatever occurs to you during the exercise is subject to discretion afterward.

Here is the structure of the Ignatian contemplation:

PRELUDES

1. Recall the actual history of what happened, remembering that the eternal Lord of all creation and the Infinite Spirit of God have entered human history in the person of Jesus Christ.

2. Use your imagination to picture the scene.

3. Ask for what I desire. Generally speaking, it will be (a) to recognize and acknowledge what Christ is doing for me; (b) to pour out my gratitude and love for him; and (c) to make concrete choices about what I will do to follow him.

POINTS

1. See the people. What have their lives been up to this point? Who are their friends? From whom do they feel alienated? What social and economic factors shape their living? With what hopes and emotions do they arrive on this scene?

2. Hear their words. Imagine all the dialog that comes before and after what Scripture reports. What tone of voice and what sort of confidence or fear can you hear?

3. See what the people do. See how their actions at this point in time have real, historical effects for you today. See how love in history works to fulfill God's plan of redemption.

4. Use your senses of smell and taste and touch to savor the tangible presence of divinity in a human scene. Consider both the external, visible actions of the persons as well as the internal movements of the Spirit of God within them.

DIALOG

Enter into dialog with the persons you have been contemplating. If this is difficult at times, imagine what would be fitting for some other person to say to these persons in this scene. Keep in mind that they are inspired by the same Spirit that inspires you with the desire to be with them.

Passages from the Hidden Life of Christ

Meditative Reading:

Hebrews 1–2. "In these last days God has spoken through his Son, through whom he made everything there is. He is the radiant light of God's glory and the perfect copy of his nature, sustaining the universe by his powerful command."

1 Jn 1:1–4. "Something which has existed since the beginning, that we have heard, . . . seen with our own eyes, . . . watched, touched with our own hands, . . . this is our subject."

Psalm 72. "Give your own justice to the king . . . that he may rule your people rightly and your poor with justice. . . . In his days virtue will flourish and a universal peace until the moon is no more. . . . He will have pity on the poor and feeble, . . . redeeming their lives from exploitation and outrage, . . . their lives will be precious in his sight."

Passages for Contemplation

1. The Incarnation. Read Phil 2:1–11, a hymn of Incarnation, how God's own Spirit, a gift of love, helps us to have the same mind as Christ Jesus.

2. Lk 1:26–38. Imagine three scenes: first, the absolute majesty of God, God's simplicity, beauty, gentleness, kindness. Second, the utter chaos of the world, with people tearing each other apart through both malice and ignorance. Third, God's surprising choice to respond to the chaos through the humility of Mary. Savor the gentle way the angel announces the conception of Jesus to Mary. See how the Spirit of God softly makes the impossible possible.

Grace: to recognize and savor the humble style in which the eternal Son becomes the human Jesus through the power of the Spirit in Mary; to love Jesus and to follow him as closely as I can.

3. Lk 1:39–56. Visitation. Relish the great joy they share together. Learn the ways in which God as Infinite Spirit works in each of them and between them.

4. Mt 1:18–25. Joseph's dread. Child to be called "Emmanuel": God is with us. The love between Joseph and Mary and how they trusted God with this strange marriage.

5. Lk 2:1–7. Mary and Joseph obey the census decree. No room in the inn. Jesus is born.

6. Jn 1:1–14. The eternal Word of God becomes human.

7. Read an Old Testament passage as Mary and Joseph would read them at this time:

Is 9:1–6. The birth of the child and the end of wars.

Psalm 63. "My soul thirsts for you, . . . my lips will recite your praise . . . for you have always helped me. . . . May those hounding me go to hell."

Psalm 131. "As a child . . . rely on the Lord always!"

8. Lk 2:8–18. Shepherds. Ask to share their humble awe and excitement.

9. Lk 2:22–38. Presentation. Jesus first comes to the Father's house. The Holy Spirit gives Simeon assurance, revelation, and prompting.

10. Mt 2:1–12. The Magi. See the prophetic signs of the gifts: gold for a king, frankincense for divinity, myrrh for death.

11. Mt 2:13–18. Flight into Egypt. Joseph's dream. The Slaughter of the Innocents. See the effects that ruthless political leaders have on the humble and the helpless. See how Mary and Joseph deal with their own fears, anger, frustrations.

12. Mt 2:19–23. Return from Egypt. Hiding, incognito. Joseph's dream (how he trusts his dreams, how well he interprets them). Return journey (Israel being called out of Egypt). See the trust that Joseph and Mary have in the midst of uncertainty and homelessness.

13. Lk 2:41–50. Finding in the temple. In the Father's house. Jesus is surprised that they wouldn't have thought to look in the temple first. Reflect on where you love to be.

14. Lk 2:39–40, 51–52. Jesus' life between twelve and twenty-eight. Jesus grew "in wisdom, age, and grace." Contemplate his obedience to Joseph and Mary. As he plies his trade as a carpenter, see how he reflects on his life.

15. The death of Joseph. Although not recorded in Scripture, it was surely an important event in the life of Jesus. Jesus surely would have read Gn 50:15–26, on the death of Joseph's namesake. Read it with Jesus. Ask Jesus why his favorite name for God is "Father."

Pull and Counterpull

As you contemplate Christ's life beginning from his decision to change its course dramatically, start to deliberate about what decision or confirmation of a decision
you need to make. To help set your decision about discipleship into the context of God's desire to bring the
Kingdom to your time and place, reflect on the following view of history.

Imagine the world. Not the planet Earth but the world
of people. Men and women, boys and girls, infants and the
elderly, the bright and the slow. Imagine not only those living but those who have died, not just recently but extending
back to generation before generation, to our earliest fore-
bears. Finally, imagine the future as it looms in the hearts
of those who love the world and the unknown children who
will inherit it.

Everyone is born of someone else. Everyone is raised by
someone else. As each person gradually wakes up from the
pangs of childbirth, he or she experiences the marvels of
self-awareness, creativity, and human concern. People tell
each other what they dreamt, what the dreams suggest,
what they hope for. Each generation thrives on the achieve-
ments of the past and suffers from its sins. Above all, people
fall in love and enlarge their self-awareness and care beyond
themselves. Their creativity finds its power and purpose in
their loyalty to tradition, in their affection for people around
them, and in their solicitude for those yet to be born.

And so the solidarity of the world continues. Human
history is a flow of events in which each turn is entirely
conditioned by the state of things immediately preceding it

and by the human capacity to direct it creatively. God made us creative and loving by nature, so that we can share in the divine act of creation motivated by love.

But the world is also, and always, a struggle. We see injustice and oppression everywhere, involving every person in one way or another. These social, economic, and political struggles have their roots in an interior struggle between obedience to the love God pours into human hearts and obedience to another love that constricts and suffocates human hearts, robbing humanity of the power that would charge its creativity.

This struggle is not like a war between superpowers, where both sides use the same strategies. Nor is it like a cold war, where both sides are relatively frozen. We experience it psychologically as a constant and sometimes violent tension between a pull and a counterpull in our consciousness.

Christian tradition has described these pulls in different ways. Far more than anyone before him, Christ talked about Satan and "the test" to which people are subjected. He laid his finger on inner desires and thoughts as the site of a person's virtue rather than on outer compliance with laws.

Augustine compared the struggle to two kings ruling over two cities: Satan over Babylon and Christ over Jerusalem. Satan rules by giving us pleasure in dominating other people and a desire to take care of ourselves above all. Christ rules by giving us a desire to love God above all and put self-concern under great suspicion.

Ignatius Loyola described Augustine's two kings in more psychological detail. Under the standard, or flag, of Satan there is the insistent pull toward being the self-made person, someone who has completely given in to the desire to control his or her own life. It starts with wanting to possess or own things—and the nicer the better. From there it develops into wanting to be esteemed, to be admired. Once we set our hearts on these honors, we commit ourselves to an "I did it my way" philosophy of life. From that pride there is hardly any evil we will not consider doing. This is because the "right thing to do" has become whatever is *for me*. The "wrong thing to do" has become whatever is *against me*.

Under the standard of Christ there is a gentler pull toward becoming the person who imitates Christ in everything. It starts with wanting to be free of attachments of material goods and being glad to imitate Christ in his own poverty. Those who experience these desires and divest themselves of certain possessions on account of them usually feel a longing to share even in the humiliations of life, the mockery of the world, and the persecution that Christ experienced. It means preferring Jesus' experience over the experiences of pleasure and security promised by our culture. We are ready to obey this pull because we believe that the human Jesus is a divine exemplar of the perfect life. More important, we are ready because of a love we experience for the crucified and risen Christ. This pull leads to a true humility about who we think we are and who God is. From that humility God very easily uses us to draw others along the same path and to letting God's will be done through us wherever we live.

What are the dynamics of these two pulls in our own culture? It is very important to understand these pulls in terms that we can verify in ourselves and in the people around us. For example, some people might see all things as gifts to be welcomed. They think of themselves as stewards of another's goods—knowing what the divine owner wants and taking great care to carry out the divine owner's desires. They conceive the opposite pull as the penchant for thinking of things as either "mine" or "theirs." Under that pull people gradually become preoccupied with possessing rather than sharing, with taking rather than giving, with self-security rather than communal life.

There are many other ways in which this dialectic of desires can manifest itself. On the side that withdraws from God it may be a desire for security or for sexual satisfaction or for power. On the side that draws toward God it is usually the opposite of the culture's dominant sin—perhaps a pull toward risk as opposed to excessive security or for genuine affectionate love rather than sexual satisfaction, or for reliance on God's Spirit for wisdom rather than on brute political power.

Consider how all the buildings and roads, all the laws and customs, all the values and ideals of our society are products of the interplay of these inner forces. As such they are ambiguous products, coming partly from people trying to take autonomous control of their lives and partly from people letting God's Spirit direct them.

In meditating on these two desires or pulls, ask for a knowledge of how the world really is structured. You are seeking not a mere acknowledgment that this is a helpful way of looking at life. Rather, you are seeking a realization, rooted in your personal experience, of what the world is really about. You are seeking what John Henry Newman calls a "real assent"—a vision of world process that you have personally verified in your own life and in the lives of the people you know.

The consequences of this realization for your own awareness of yourself and others are profound. You will grow more keenly aware of the two pulls in your own life, which is a lifelong process of learning. And you will listen to others with a new ear, one attuned to the pull and counterpull behind what they say. You will gradually learn how to respond to their real interiors, as one heart speaks to another.

Keep your focus on "sin in the world" rather than on your own sin. Although the dialectic of desires works out in a way peculiar to each person, and each one of us has a particular pattern of traps to avoid, the point here is to envision the world with the apostolic desires of God's Infinite Spirit.

It will be a great help here to ask the intercession of the Blessed Mother. Her vocation, like yours, was to bring the Word of God to the world. You share in her Motherhood in a manner very unique to your time and place.

Given the fact that we no longer consider persons sheerly in universal, abstract terms but rather in terms of the meanings and values that shape their actual living, it will also help to discuss with others what might be the dominant pulls and counterpulls at work in your culture today. A shared theology of history will be very helpful in exploring an apostolic vision with others.

Test your view of this dialectic of history by seeing it as the work of both Christ and the Spirit. Who is Christ for your concrete situation? Christ the Stranger? Christ the Compassion of God? Christ the Teacher? Christ the Companion of the Poor? In what ways does the Spirit of God in Christ "groan in a great act of childbirth"? For justice? For companionship? For wisdom? How does the Spirit cry out "Abba!" where you live?

Also, ask for the grace to feel *drawn* or *pulled* toward the love of God. You are not making a commitment here to follow Christ. You are asking to experience the concrete desires that flow from loving God—desires to take risks, to live simply, to obey within. You are asking to experience these desires not in passing but in a way that governs your everyday choices.

From this point on in the Second Week, set all the meditations against the background of this view of history. As you take each meditation, beg to experience the pull, the desire, to love God in a way that allows the Spirit to work freely through you to redeem your situation. Insist on receiving a confirmation, an inner assurance, that God does put you at Christ's side, sharing his Spirit under the standard of his cross.

As a help to making this vision your own, reflect on the parable of the "Two Standards" as found in Ignatius' *Spiritual Exercises* included here.

The Two Standards

PRELUDES

1. Recall the actual history of world events. In particular, recall that Christ desires and invites every person into the Kingdom. Lucifer, by contrast, desires every person's destruction, urging them into a life of hell.

2. Imagine a great plain around Jerusalem, where the commander-in-chief of all good people is Christ our Lord. Imagine another plain around Babylon, where the chief of the enemy is Lucifer.

3. Ask for what I desire. Here it will be to ask for a firm knowledge of the deceits of the rebel chief and to help guard myself against them; and also to ask for a firm knowledge of the true life exemplified in the sovereign and true Commander and the grace to imitate him.

PART ONE: THE STANDARD OF SATAN

1. Imagine you see the chief of all the enemy in a vast plain around Babylon, seated on a great throne of fire and smoke—a terrifying and horrible figure.

2. Consider how he gathers countless demons, and how he scatters them, some to one city and some to another, throughout the whole world, so that no province, no place, no state of life, not a single individual is overlooked.

3. Consider the address he makes to them, and how he goads them on to lay snares and cast various chains. First they are to tempt people to desire riches, in most cases, which draws them on to the empty honors of the world and finally to an overweening pride.

So the first step will be riches, the second honor, the third pride. From these three steps he leads people to all the other vices.

PART TWO: THE STANDARD OF CHRIST

1. In a similar but opposite way, imagine you see the sovereign and true Commander, Christ our Lord. Consider how he takes his stand on a great plain around Jerusalem, in a humble place, fair and gracious.

2. Consider how the Lord of the entire world chooses so many persons—apostles, disciples, and so on—and sends them throughout the whole world to spread his holy teaching to all people, no matter what their state or condition.

3. Consider the address Christ our Lord makes to all his servants and friends whom he sends on this enterprise. He instructs them to be ready to help anyone and everyone, leading them first to the highest spiritual poverty and, if it pleases the Divine Majesty and should God so choose them, to an actual poverty. Second, they should lead people to a desire for reproaches and contempt because it is from these that humility springs.

There are three steps. The first is poverty as opposed to riches. The second is reproaches and contempt as opposed to worldly honor. The third is humility as opposed to pride. From these three steps they are to lead people to all the other virtues.

DIALOG

Enter into conversation with Our Lady, begging to obtain for you the grace from her Son and our Lord that you may be received under his standard, first in the highest spiritual poverty and, if it pleases the Divine Majesty and should God so choose to receive you, no less in actual poverty; second, in bearing all insults and injuries in order to imitate him better, provided only that you can suffer these without sin on the part of another and without offense to the Divine Majesty. End with a *Hail Mary*.

Ask the same of the Son to obtain the same experience from the Father. End with the following prayer: "Lord Jesus Christ, Son of the Living God, by the will of the Father and the work of the Spirit, your death brought life to our world. By your holy Body and Blood, free me from all my sins and from every evil. Keep me faithful to your teaching. And never let me be parted from you."

Ask the same from the Father. End with an *Our Father*.

Meditative Reading:

Eph 6:10–20. "Grow strong in the Lord.... Resist the devil's tactics.... Spread the good news of peace.... Keep praying in the Spirit on every occasion."

Gal 5:16–25. "If you are guided by the Spirit there will be no danger of self-indulgence. What the Spirit brings: love, joy, peace, patience, kindness, goodness, trustfulness, gentleness, and self-control."

Jas 1:2–8. "Treat your trials as a happy privilege, ... patience has a practical result—you will become fully-developed, complete, with nothing missing. If you need wisdom, ask God, who gives to all freely and ungrudgingly; it will be given to you. But ask without doubt.... The person who wavers between going different ways must not expect that the Lord will give anything."

Passages from the Public Life of Christ

To keep your focus on who Jesus is that you are contemplating, and who the Spirit is that brings you to Jesus, use one or another of the three texts below to begin your contemplation. These texts all show that Jesus is God's most personal and irrevocable Word. Jesus is the "Christ," which means "the Anointed," the one with God's own charism, God's own Spirit. Any restlessness you feel for "God" will be comforted only in Jesus. You can count on the Holy Spirit to bring you to Jesus.

Col 1:15–20. Christ is the head of all creation. He holds all things in unity. All things are reconciled through him and for him.

Phil 2:1–11. The Holy Spirit urges you to have the mind of Christ who emptied himself, became human, yet humbler.

Eph 1:3–14. Blessed be God the Father, who chose us before the world was made to live in Christ. You have heard the good news and been stamped with the seal of the Holy Spirit.

The Scripture texts that follow are arranged roughly chronologically but under various topics. This is to facilitate choosing passages that may better match where the Spirit has led you in retreat.

Jesus Receives the Spirit at Baptism.

Grace: to experience a share in Jesus' knowledge that he is especially beloved of the Father.

1. Jesus chooses to leave mother, occupation, home. He is moved by the Spirit to go to the Jordan, where John is baptizing. Walk with him.

2. Jn 1:29–39. John the Baptist points clearly to Jesus as the giver of the Holy Spirit. Jn 3:27–36. "A person can lay claim only to what is given from heaven. . . . The joy I feel is now complete. He must grow greater, I must grow smaller."

3. Mk 1:9–11. Jesus' baptism: Jesus accepts his identity as Beloved from God, whose love and favor are given as the Spirit descends on Jesus. His commitment to his choice of a way of life.

Grace: to desire to be called by the Father to an evangelical way of life in this same manner—by welcoming God's love and favor through accepting the Holy Spirit.

The Spirit Leads Jesus into the Wilderness.

Grace: to welcome the fact that Jesus shares even in being a victim of temptation; to recognize what strategies Satan uses to draw me away from God's purposes.

1. Mt 4:1–11. Jesus' temptation. Watch how the Spirit leads Jesus into the wilderness. Notice how the devil does not tempt Jesus to sin or give in to weakness but to use his strengths for personal security, honor, power.
Grace: to be realistic about coming temptations, particularly temptations that divert my energies from making a total commitment to God's calling; to feel confidence in God's help at that time.

The Spirit Impels Jesus to Teach.

Grace: to welcome the teaching of Jesus as my absolute guide to life.

1. Lk 4:16–22. Jesus' first preaching at Nazareth. "Jesus, with the power of the Spirit in him, returned to Galilee." See how the Spirit inspires Jesus.

2. Mt 5:1–48. The Beatitudes.
Grace: to know not only what Jesus teaches but to share in the Spirit that knows what to teach. For repetitions or continuations, see Mt 6:1–34; 7:1–5, 21–27; Lk 6:20–49; 11:1–13; 12:1–12, 22–34.

Jesus Is Rejected.

Grace: to learn from Jesus how to keep my heart set on God when someone rejects me.

1. Lk 4:23–30. Jesus' first experience of rejection.

2. Lk 13:31–35. Jesus told by the Pharisees to leave. Jesus weeps over Jerusalem's refusal to be gathered as chicks are gathered by a hen.

Jesus Calms the Storms.

Grace: to feel the peace that Jesus brings and to rely on his strength when storms come.

1. Mt 8:23–27. Calming of the storm.

2. Mt 14:22–33. Jesus walks on the water.

Jesus Heals.

See analogies in the present day for each of the many afflictions Jesus has compassion for.

Grace: to acknowledge Jesus' power to heal me; to feel great desire to heal with Jesus.

1. Mk 1:21–28. Jesus' first miracle after the temptation is to assert his power over all evil spirits.

2. Jn 5:1–9. Sick man at the pool, waiting for an angel to move the water. "Do you want to be healed?"

3. Mk 10:46–52. Bartimaeus, the blind beggar, shouts for help and will not be silenced. "What do you want me to do for you?"

4. Lk 13:10–17. Woman unable to stand upright for eighteen years. See Jesus' great compassion and desire to free a person from Satan's bondage.

5. Lk 8:43–48. Woman with hemorrhage for twelve years reaches out gingerly to Jesus.

Jesus Calls Me by Name.

The Spirit in Jesus loves you, and the Spirit in you loves Jesus.

Grace: to know that Jesus calls me by name and in all truth desires intently that I walk with him.

1. Lk 19:1–10. Zacchaeus climbs down from his sycamore tree and joyfully begins a new way of life.

2. Jn 11:38–44. Jesus raises Lazarus, releases him from bondage, gives him a freedom to face death.

3. Mt 16:13–18, 23. Jesus calls Simon, who will often be weak and afraid; his faults show even after Pentecost (avoids Gentiles and is rebuked by Paul).

Grace: to know that you are called *with* your weaknesses.

4. Lk 7:36–50. Conversion of Magdalene. See how she expresses her faith in Jesus.

Grace: to experience a deep and moving love for Jesus.

5. Acts 9:1–9. Jesus calls Saul, gives him directives only for the next step. He is blind to everything for a while.

Grace: to accept Jesus' call even if I cannot see where it will lead; to accept my blindness.

Jesus Challenges Me.

Grace: to face my fears about responding to Jesus' invitation and to bring them explicitly to Jesus, begging for courage to respond.

1. Mi 6:8. "This is all the Lord asks of you: to act justly, to love tenderly, and to walk humbly with your God." Feel your desire to live your entire life on these simple principles.

2. Lk 9:57–62. Several want to follow, but not immediately. What excuses do you have for putting off a decision to follow?

3. Mk 10:17–27. A rich young man, very obedient, whom Jesus looks upon with love, walks away when Jesus invites him to give all he has to the poor and follow him.

Resting in the Company of Jesus.

Grace: to relish the company of Jesus; to experience the Spirit's work of simple, loving welcome; to gain an interior knowledge of "the one thing necessary."

1. Jn 1:35–51. The call of Andrew and the beloved disciple. "'What do you want?' ... 'Where do you dwell?' ... 'Come and see.' They went, they saw where he dwelt, they dwelt with him the rest of that day."

2. Jn 2:1–12. Cana. Jesus offers a rich, new wine. Mary says, "Do whatever he tells you."

3. Mt 11:25–30. "I praise you Father for revealing these things to little ones. . . . Come to me all who are burdened."

4. Lk 10:38–41. "Martha, you fret about many things, only one thing is necessary, and Mary has chosen the better part; it is not going to be taken from her."

5. Jn 6:30–44. "I am the bread of life, never be hungry. Whoever comes to me I shall not turn away."

6. Jn 15:1–20. Vine and branches. Consider how you are one of many branches stretching throughout all history.

Grace: to realize how God desires the whole human race to be attached to the divine Word in history through the divine Spirit of love in hearts.

7. Jn 13:1–17. Jesus washes the feet of the disciples.

8. Jn 12:1–10. Mary anoints the feet of Jesus and wipes them with her hair.

   Grace: to feel Mary's loving compassion for Jesus as he approaches his suffering and death.

End of Second Week.

1. Mt 17:1–9. Transfiguration. "My Son, the Beloved." Moses and Elija represent the entire Law and Prophets. "Stand up. Do not be afraid. When they raised their eyes, they saw no one but only Jesus."

Third Week

"Jerusalem, Jerusalem!"

The Spirit of Compassion

During this Week you will seek the spiritual consolation of sorrow with Christ sorrowful. What is his profound sorrow? "Jerusalem, Jerusalem, you that kill the prophets and stone those who are sent to you! How often have I longed to gather your children, as a hen gathers her chicks under her wings, and you refused!" (Mt 23:37–33).

Notice that this means understanding *why* Jesus is sorrowful and sharing in those feelings of sorrow. It is a Week to befriend sorrow. A Week of immersion in the experience of God as God embraces the suffering of the world. It is a shared pity for God's people.

Ask for the grace not to forget suffering, ever. If we forget the genocides, the public horrors of war and secret horrors of oppressive dictatorships, the ravages of drugs and abuse in families, then we think of both the lives and the deaths of our brothers and sisters as meaningless. We have no message to offer the living. Freedom, liberation, justice, happiness—just words whose concrete meaning has drained out of them. Ask for the grace to remember, to carry the death of the Human deep in your heart.

To recall death in ourselves and in our brothers and sisters does not mean ignoring any pity for Jesus as you recall how he was tortured and killed. On the contrary, to focus on his sufferings means to learn about the mystery of love in the one person who died perfectly for love. Let yourself feel helpless to help Christ, except to spend the time witnessing and remembering his own terrible losses. As God freely chose, out of love, to be bound irrevocably to human mortality, so you can freely choose to accompany Jesus irrevocably in his Passion.

As you accompany him you will discover that he in fact is accompanying you. You do not so much need to achieve a sense of Christ's sufferings as to let the suffering Christ accompany you in your suffering. Let yourself be the object of Christ's compassion, particularly insofar as you are part of some Jerusalem today. Christ still weeps over the churches, the businesses, the hospitals, the schools, the governments—not so much because of human frailty as because of their refusal to treat all men and women as God's beloved. Consider how Christ weeps over your communities, how he longs for them to share the joy of reconciling people to one another and bringing justice to the world, and how much pity he feels for the destruction they bring upon themselves.

Make every effort to bring yourself just as you are. Do not hide any aspect of your mortality from him who freely chose to face death with you. Bring your own deepest fears. Bring anything that makes you anxious. Bring any frustrations, resentments, and anger to Jesus in the scene you are contemplating.

In particular, bring the decision you made in the Second Week to every exercise, not to deliberate about it further but to confirm it in the context of love-unto-death. You will walk with Jesus toward Jerusalem, all the way to the cross, as a person who has made a serious and concrete commitment to enter the paschal mystery in your particular circumstances. While you seek the consolation of shared sorrow and tears with Christ, be prepared also to experience the desolation of dryness and apparent aimlessness. Don't give in to self-pity. Fight against the desolation. Work against any self-preoccupation and focus instead on what the Father is doing, what the Spirit is doing in Jesus and in you, and what Jesus is doing and why he is doing it. Do not analyze yourself as if you were alone. When you call to mind your own weakness, always do so in the company of Jesus and with the desires only of the Holy Spirit.

Even though you should courageously act against spiritual desolation, there are several ways to accept it while it is with you.

- Accept it as a sacrament of your own mortality, your own personal limitations and weakness. It is a sign that we cannot find life except in God.

- Accept it also as a share in Christ's own desolation: "Father why have you forsaken me?" It is a great mystery that God hides the divinity from those who are about to embody it most concretely.

- Accept it as a share in the Spirit's own agony: "Not only creation, but all of us who possess the first-fruits of the Spirit, we too groan inwardly as we wait for our bodies to be set free" (Rom 8:23).

- Accept it, finally, in solidarity with your brothers and sisters throughout the world and throughout history. It is your share in the chief question about God that the majority of people ask: Why do we suffer unjustly?

During the Third Week use any one of the following texts to orient yourself:

1 Pt 1:3–12. A cause of joy, even though for a short time you are plagued by all sorts of trials. Your faith will have been tested and proved like gold. The Spirit of Christ in the prophets foretold the sufferings of Christ and the glories that would follow. Even angels long to catch a glimpse of these things.

1 Pt 4:12–19. Be glad if you have a share in the sufferings of Christ. You have the Spirit of glory, the Spirit of God resting on you. Do not be ashamed to suffer for being a Christian; those whom God allows to suffer must trust themselves to the constancy of the Creator and go on doing good.

2 Cor 1:3–7. A gentle Father who comforts us in all our sorrows, so that we can offer others, in their sorrows, the consolation that we have received from God ourselves.

2 Cor 4:7–18. We are only earthenware jars. We carry with us in our body the death of Jesus, so that the life of Jesus, too, may always be seen in our body. Our troubles train us for the carrying of a weight of eternal glory which is all out of proportion to them.

Rom 8:14–27. Everyone moved by the Spirit is a child of God, making us cry, "Abba, Father!" We are coheirs with Christ, sharing his sufferings so as to share his glory.

Rom 8:28–39. Even if we are troubled or worried, or being persecuted, or lacking food or clothes, or being threatened or even attacked, nothing can come between us and God's love for us made visible in Christ Jesus our Lord.

2 Cor 11:23–31. I have worked and labored, often without sleep; I have been hungry and thirsty and often starving; I have been in the cold without clothes. If I am to boast, then let me boast of my own feebleness.

Phil 3:5–13. All I want is to know Christ and the power of his resurrection and to share his sufferings by reproducing the pattern of his death.

Col 2:6–7; 3:1–4. You must be rooted in him and built on him and held firm by the faith you have been taught, and full of thanksgiving.

You may find it helpful to listen to Handel's *Messiah* or Bach's *St. Matthew's Passion*.

The Law of the Cross

The Law of the Cross is not just an opaque principle of nature—"Unless the seed fall to the ground and die, it will not produce fruit." It is an intelligible principle of love—that self-concern blocks our compassion for others.

In the agonies of Jesus and the Spirit, God uncovers the central meaning of love for us, how love is essentially connected with sin and death. The crucifixion reveals to us that it is better to suffer evil than to do evil. But we do not really grasp the meaning of this mystery of love-unto-death unless we contemplate the actual events in the life of Jesus and relate them to the actual deaths in ourselves and in our brothers and sisters.

It may help, as a background to the contemplations of this week, to recall five ways in which we touch sin and death. In each way we find the mystery of love.

1. There is our own physical deaths, as well as our physical diseases, psychological illnesses, and the losses we incur through the happenstances of nature and history. These can be extremely painful, or the pain can be deadly slow and drawn out, gradually eroding all our joy and trust. But they are not sins. They may be the result of someone's sin, but they cannot introduce the evil of sin into our hearts without our free consent. Still, they do rob our hope and perseverance and are evil in the sense that they heighten the chances that our weakness surpasses our moral strength. The evil of physical deaths lies in how they condition us for moral death. In other words, the central meaning of physical deaths is their power to make sin easy.

2. The only true personal death is sin. Far beyond any physical suffering, in which we may lose a limb or eyesight, beyond our own physical deaths, far beyond even the loss of one's best friend, sin is the loss of the finest part of our own selves. Its evil can be fathomed only by witnessing the response to sin by God in Christ Jesus, since once sin enters our souls it assures us that all is well. When we sin, sin lives and we die.

3. When physical deaths threaten our souls and we resist, then sin dies and we live. This happens when we turn the other cheek or suppress a hurtful comment. To live in a nonretaliatory and generous fashion means death to our egos. Everyone who cares actively for others and reconciles people with one another dies to self in this manner.

4. We symbolize these three deaths in baptism—not a sign of cleansing but of dying to sin and rising to genuine life. By baptism we state to the world and to ourselves that we reject the evil of sin even in the face of the greatest physical evils and moral deaths. Likewise, in the Eucharist we "recall the death of the Lord until he comes." That is, we reenter the paschal mystery with Jesus by eating and drinking as he commanded us.

5. Finally, there is the death of asceticism or self-denial. Ascetism is a life-giving habit on several fronts.

First, by penance or self-denial we deepen our solidarity with the world loved by God. In other words, as we gradually put to death our concern to avoid suffering at all costs, we experience the resurrection of a readiness to walk with those who suffer. We begin to feel the new life of the blessed poor in spirit, part of the great act of childbirth that all creation is undergoing, crying "Abba! Father!"

Second, we grow in spiritual attentiveness to inner experience when we die to material concerns. Penance not only robs gross temptations of their power, it attunes us to distinguish between good and better.

Third, we grow in identification with Jesus, who freely chose human mortality out of divine compassion. When all other reasons for self-denial seem unconvincing, it helps greatly to recall that when God freely chose to give the divine self to us perfectly, Jesus and the Spirit came to suffer our mortality and our malice.

On all three fronts, however, what makes them life giving is not mere passion but compassion. Any self-denial without compassion verges dangerously on self-justification or, what is worse, self-punishment.

Structure of
the Exercises

PRELUDES

1. The eternal God, whom we long to see and adore face to face, has entered human history in the person of Jesus and in the divine Spirit offered to every human being. God groans and suffers in this work to redeem history.

2. Imagine the setting and approach with awe and respect. Filled with the Holy Spirit, Jesus will reveal the true nature of love—at times wonderful but at times terrifying. Thus the mystery of God's own compassionate and awe-inspiring self is revealed in the particular scene I am about to contemplate.

3. Ask for what I desire. During the Third Week, it will be to ask (1) for an intimate understanding of Jesus' great sorrow over the impending self-destruction of his people; (2) a grasp of the full nature of true love as exemplified in Jesus' compassionate Spirit; and (3) an abiding realization that the Lord of all creation and history chooses to redeem it by entering it permanently—that is, to realize within myself that this is true and to let my emotions react to this reality.

POINTS

In each of these points, see the persons, particularly where they come from, what histories they bear, what families and communities they represent, with what hope or dejection they arrive. Hear the dialog between them and feel the sorrow and anguish in their voices. Watch their actions, seeing what grief does to them. See each of them struggle to be free from fear yet still afraid.

1. Consider how Jesus experiences the Holy Spirit prompting him to enter into the sufferings of others. Consider his mental and spiritual anguish as well as his physical pain. Make a strong effort to grieve, to be sad, to weep with Jesus over the people he weeps over.

2. Consider how Christ's divinity hides itself. He is less and less attractive, charismatic, miraculous. Full of spiritual desolation, Christ himself feels bereft: "My God, my God, why have you abandoned me?"

3. Consider how the Father brings Jesus to this point for love of the human family, so that each person, like you, might feel God's healing love in his or her own historical situation. Beg the eternal Word Incarnate to give you an understanding of his own compassionate love for you through those who care for you. Reflect on how you should be ready to carry on the compassion of Jesus in your own time and place.

DIALOG

Be ready to enter into conversation with the persons in the scene you are contemplating. Be particularly ready to talk about the suffering people in each of your lives—those they love and care for, those you love and care for. Speak to God and hear God's Word as he speaks, and feel God's Spirit as it cries out. During this week the dialogs should be laden with grief and sorrow. Beg for the kind of grief and sorrow that binds you to Jesus (and is therefore a spiritual consolation) rather than the kind that pulls you away from him, away from those who suffer and into yourself. Bring the commitment you made in the Second Week to Jesus, particularly the losses it involves.

Meditative Reading:

Each of these passages is about the events leading up to the Passion and death of Jesus. They will help you understand the thoughts and feelings of Jesus as he approaches his death.

Matthew 21–25. Entrance into Jerusalem. Drives out money changers. Signs against hard-hearted Jews: curses barren tree; parables of two sons, of wicked tenants, of wedding feast. Further traps of Pharisees, of scribes. The two great commandments. Indictment of scribes and Pharisees. Eschatological discourse.

Jn 11:55–12:50. Anointing at Bethany. Entrance into Jerusalem. "What shall I say: Father, save me from this hour? But it was for this very reason that I have come to this hour. Father, glorify your name!" "Whoever believes in me need not stay in the dark any more."

Lk 21:5–22:46 (or Mk 13–14:42). Predictions of the destruction of temple, of Christians, of Jerusalem. Be alert for the Coming of Son of Man. Conspiracy against Jesus. Last Supper. Gethsemane.

Lk 10:41–44. Jesus weeps over Jerusalem.

Scriptural Passages

1. Jn 12:1–11. Anointing at Bethany. Feel Mary's compassion for Jesus.

2. Heb 5:1–10. He offered up prayer and entreaty, aloud and in silent tears, to the one who had the power to save him out of death. Although Son, he learned to obey through suffering.

3. Mt 26:20–30. Last Supper. Feel the great and tender love Jesus has for the friends who will be lost without him.

4. Jn 13:1–30. Washing of the feet. See how greatly Jesus desires that they imitate his service to others.

5. Jn 13:33–14:7. Farewell discourse: "I shall not be with you much longer. . . . A new commandment: love one another as I have loved you. . . . Do not let your hearts be troubled. . . . I am going now to prepare a place for you."

6. Jn 14:8–31. Farewell discourse: "To have seen me is to have seen the Father. . . . Ask anything in my name and I will do it. . . . I will not leave you orphans. . . . My peace I give you."

7. Mt 26:30–46. Peter's denial predicted. Agony in the Garden. What really is Jesus' greatest agony here? Ask him.

8. Mt 26:47–56. Arrest. See in Jesus all the men and women arrested and imprisoned.

9. Mt 26:57–68. Jesus taken to Caiaphas. Feel the confrontation between worldly authority, with all its lies and tricks, and one person standing firm in the truth.

10. Mt 26:69–75. Peter's denials. Ask for the grace to feel for Peter exactly as Jesus does. And that the grace abide in anyone you know who is betrayed.

11. Lk 23:6–12. Jesus before Herod. See the horror in the way people can enjoy themselves and become friends over a common hatred.

12. Mt 27:11–26. Jesus before Pilate and the crowd. See the terrible irony in the crowd asking that Jesus' blood be on them and on their children.

13. Mt 27:27–31. Torture. Jesus, true King in the Kingdom of God, is mocked. Seek to understand how Jesus sees their souls.

14. Acts 2:14–36. Peter describes Jesus in his agony as reciting Psalm 16. Read Psalm 16 and hear it as Jesus might say it. Also, read Psalm 22, which Matthew (27:46) sees Jesus as crying out on the cross. Or recite these psalms for Jesus, as if he were too weak to pray aloud but asked you to pray the words for him.

15. The crucifixion and burial of Jesus (Mt 27:32–66) may be prayed over very simply. Perhaps spend an entire day on these events, silently absorbing their significance. There is no need to achieve anything here. You already have been united to Jesus and to all people in history simply through your own mortality. Let today be a sign that you have accepted Christ's victory over any fear of any death that has ever gripped you. Let today be a confirmation of your desire to take away the fears of the many deaths your brothers and sisters face.

16. John 17–19. Presents the crucifixion and burial with more emphasis on the fearlessness and triumph of Jesus.

THE SABBATH DAY

A time to rest in mourning. Read the four Suffering Servant songs of Isaiah, with special emphasis on the fourth. Hear especially the love the Servant has for his people. Imagine hearing Mary read them on Good Friday night. Ask for an intimate understanding of the fact that Jesus really died and of how the disciples experienced it, as a loss not merely of a friend but of a hope for Israel.

Is 42:1–9
Is 49:1–6
Is 50:4–11
Is 52:13–53:12

THE FIRST DAY

This will be a day of quiet rest from the previous Week and a preparation for the Fourth Week.

Read the first preaching of God lifting up Jesus to life—Acts 2:14–36; 3:12–26; 4:8–12. Imagine yourself as a hearer of this word. Seek to understand exactly what Peter understands about the Resurrection (rather than reading in what you might already think about it). Let your hopes for humanity rise. Let your heart joyfully anticipate the coming Week, when you will hear the various stories of Jesus' appearances to his disciples.

Fourth Week

"Peace be with you!"

The Spirit of
Forgiveness

Faith is required to notice and savor the joy of this Week. Approach it as a *learner,* as if you don't know exactly what this joy is. It is not joy that the retreat is nearly over. If that's what you feel, then count it a desolation. It is not a feeling of such triumph that you doubt you will ever be in desolation again. You will again be brought to your knees wondering why God has abandoned you. It is not even joy that Jesus does not suffer anymore. Jesus continues to suffer in his body, the human race, and in you personally. Nor is it a joy that forgets the suffering of the present world and the atrocities of the past.

Rather, it is a share in the joy of Jesus that death, particularly the fear of death and all forms of self-loss, need no longer be the driving force of human living. A new Kingdom has been established. A Kingdom in which the eye of love sees new possibilities and forgives old offenses. Jesus is joyful because he knows that this has been the Father's eternal desire. It is a joy one friend has for another. It is your personal joy at having experienced with Jesus the full breadth of the paschal mystery and now experience a confidence that you will live out that mystery as a companion of Jesus.

Just as you have shared in the compassion of Jesus for the world, so now you will enter into a permanent sharing in the joy of Jesus. But there is a strange phenomenon to notice about the consolation of the Fourth Week: we can *fear* this consolation because we know it has great power to move us beyond where we feel secure. Deep down we know how much control we will be giving up. Pray to be malleable.

It is very important to recall three dogmas here. First, Jesus did not come back to life as Lazarus did. Scripture does not present Jesus as "getting up again," as if he were asleep. He truly died just as any human being dies. Still less is the Resurrection a miracle done by Jesus. The Easter message is "God raised this man Jesus to life, . . . and raised to the heights by God's right hand, he has received from the Father the Holy Spirit, who was promised, and what you see is the outpouring of that Spirit. . . . God has made this Jesus whom you crucified both Lord and Christ" (Acts 2:32–36). The narratives focus on a number of preternatural appearances in which Jesus reveals his person, his mission, and his assurances to those who believe in him.

Second, Luke and John give very different accounts of how the Holy Spirit was given to the disciples. For John it occurred on Easter Sunday evening; for Luke it was after a forty-day instruction period. Whatever the historical chronology was, in reality it is always the Spirit in us who recognizes and welcomes the Son. Keep in mind that the joy you desire to share with Jesus is the work of Jesus' own Spirit in you.

Third, the good news is essentially that God is now giving us the same new life that Jesus has. "The savior we are waiting for will transfigure these wretched bodies of ours into copies of his glorious body. He will do that by the same power with which he can subdue the whole universe" (Phil 3:21). "Though our outer nature is wasting away, our inner nature is being renewed every day" (2 Cor 4:16). So the events you contemplate are as much about our common human nature as about God's work in Jesus.

Be moderate in your eating and sleeping; no penance. During this Week of exercises, read the following:

Paul's letter to Philippians

Colossians

2 Corinthians

Revelation 4–5

1 John

The "Contemplations to Experience Love" (p. 115) are excellent exercises to make for the days and weeks following the retreat. They keep you in an abiding spirit of gratitude and great liberality with the Lord. They reinforce your love of others as fellow members of the Kingdom. If you choose, you might begin them during this Week.

Structure of
the Exercises

PRELUDES

1. The eternal God, who longs to show the divine self to us, raises Jesus up, giving him the name above all names ("Lord") and reveals him as Lord to the disciples on a number of different occasions.

2. Imagine the setting and approach with peace and deep joy.

3. Ask for what I desire. During the Fourth Week it will be to ask to share in the Lord Jesus' own joy and peace. That is, I am joyful chiefly because Jesus is joyful. That is how friends are. And Jesus is joyful because the Reign of God has now begun in history. I also ask for an intimate knowledge of how my life—with the actual joys I experience— is joy with Christ, is a direct experience of Jesus' own Holy Spirit, and will be an enduring share in the paschal mystery.

POINTS

In each of these points, see the persons, particularly where they come from, what histories they bear, what social boundaries limit them, with what hope or dejection they arrive. Hear the dialog between them and listen to the joy and peace in their voices. Watch their actions, how they radiate joyfulness and peace.

1. Consider what divinity looks like in the flesh. Jesus is more and more radiant and attractive to others. He is neither anxious nor afraid. He knows himself as completely and forever human and yet the perfect revelation of God and filled with God as Spirit. See how divinity appears in human form. Reflect on how divinity radiates from you.

2. Watch how Jesus acts as consoler, bringer of peace, full of reassurance for his friends. See this peace as Jesus' gift of the Spirit. Compare it to how friends do this for one another. Let him console you in your deepest fears and pain.

3. Consider how Jesus is still a human and forever will be. He still bears the wounds of his death. Meditate on what this means for how you regard your own humanity.

4. Consider how Jesus is Lord of all creation and how his Infinite Spirit hovers over the chaos to bring peace, that is, the meaning and purpose of human history are to be found in Jesus and his Spirit. Call to mind the paschal mystery as it shows in all human agony, endeavor, birth, death, and hope.

DIALOG

Speak with Jesus as friend to friend. Or speak with Mary, then Jesus, then the Father. Invite the Spirit to move your heart to the words and deeds of love. Or speak with the Trinity, beginning with Jesus or the Holy Spirit and then the Father, remembering that they share a single mind and will and heart, so that the Spirit is our Creator, the Word is our Creator, and their Source is our Creator. Let the peace of Christ fill the commitment you made during the Second Week.

Scriptural Passages

Appearances of Jesus.

You might intersperse contemplations of the appearances of the risen Jesus with meditations on their meaning in the next section, "The Meaning of the Resurrection."

1. Jn 20:1–10. Peter and John at the tomb. John believes.

2. Jn 20:11–18 or Mt 28:1–9. Appears to Mary Magdalene. Says her name. He is going to her Father as well as his. Share the joy of Mary. The first two believers in the risen Jesus are those who love him most tenderly.

3. Jn 20:19–23. Appears to the disciples on Easter evening and sends them exactly as the Father sent him. He then gives them his Holy Spirit to bring forgiveness to one another. Feel the peace of the gathering.

4. Jn 21:1–14. Appears at dawn on the shore of Lake Tiberius. Note the sign he gives them: an abundance of whatever they were fishing for.

5. Lk 24:13–35. Appears to two disciples on road to Emmaus. He eats with his friends. Explains the paschal mystery. As soon as he is recognized he no longer needs to be seen.

6. Lk 24:36–43. Jesus appears to the eleven and their companions. Eats a piece of grilled fish. Their recognition is not sudden but gradual.

7. Lk 24:44–53. Jesus commissions the eleven and their companions. As he withdraws from them they are full of joy. There is never nostalgia for Jesus.

8. Jn 21:15–19. Christ forgives and commissions Peter. Notice how, beginning from verse 1, the story is a complete vignette of the life of Peter, with his denials reversed. What vignette would represent your discipleship?

9. Jn 20:24–29. Thomas needs evidence. Jesus appears a second time to disciples, when Thomas is present. Thomas believes. Calls Jesus "Lord" and "God." Notice that Jesus still carries his wounds, just as you will for eternity. What wounds will be your victory?

10. Mt 28:16–20. Jesus appears to the eleven disciples. Sends them to make disciples of all peoples.

11. Acts 9:1–19. The living Jesus appears to Paul.

12. Eight questions of Jesus in John's Gospel:

    Why are you crying? (20:15)

    Who is it you are looking for? (20:16)

    Do you believe because you see me? (20:29)

    Haven't you caught anything? (21:5)

    Do you love me more than these others? (21:15)

    Do you love me? (21:16)

    Do you like me? (21:17)

    If I want him to live until I come, what is that to you?
    (21:22)

The Meaning of the Resurrection.

These passages cast light on the Gospel narratives. You might intersperse these with contemplations of the appearances of Jesus.

1. Jn 14:18–29. Jesus promises to return and live in the disciples through love.

2. Lk 9:28–36. Transfiguration. This is an appearance much like the Easter appearances—showing Jesus to be the fulfillment of the Law (Moses) and Prophets (Elijah).

3. 1 Cor 15:20–28. The new Head of the human race. We are in solidarity through our mortality, and now in solidarity through the new life of love, building a Kingdom in history that Christ will hand over to the Father. Contemplate this in the context of the "pull and counterpull" vision of history.

The Gift of the Spirit.

The ultimate sign and proof that Jesus is indeed the Christ sent by God to inaugurate a Reign of praise, justice, and peace is that the long-expected Spirit would be given to the people as a whole.

1. Jl 3:1–5. The promise of the Holy Spirit to be given to all God's people. Feel the hope for that day that Israelites felt.

2. Acts 2:1–21. Pentecost. See how the Spirit breaks all social boundaries.

3. Jn 16:5–15. Jesus explains about the work of the Spirit.

4. Acts 10:44–48. The Spirit comes upon listeners. See how the Spirit comes upon the unlikely, those considered beyond the pale.

5. 1 Cor 12:1–11. Gifts of the Spirit. See how the Spirit gives many different gifts, all coming to a unity of purpose.

6. 1 Cor 13:1–13. The gift of love.

7. Gal 5:16–26. The fruits of the Spirit. See the fruits the Spirit gives everyone: love, joy, peace, patience, kindness, goodness, trustfulness, gentleness, and self-control. Reflect on how these work to bring order out of chaos and how they stop cycles of oppression.

8. Revelation 21–22. The Lord appears on Judgment Day. The Spirit and the Bride say, "Come!"

PART II

Other Exercises

Contemplations to Experience Love

"Listen, Israel, the Lord our God is the one Lord, and you must love the Lord your God with all your heart, with all your soul, with all your mind and with all your strength. The second is this: You must love your neighbor as yourself" (Mk 12:30).

There are two sets of contemplations here, one set to experience love for God and the other to experience love for your neighbor. These are meant to be nontaxing exercises, using imagination and feeling, simply to allow your love to surface and let all other concerns recede. They can be made for very brief periods or for longer periods. Plan to make them often.

There are three things to remember about love, however. First, the test of genuine love is the desire to act. Good will is not enough. Even the words of love are inappropriate; what counts is deeds. So enter into these exercises with the desire and expectation that they will dispose you to act in some concrete, loving way.

Second, love does more than give something to the beloved; love also joins the beloved in a spirit of common purpose. Love not only takes care and gives, love joins and shares. So in these exercises be prepared not only to act but to act in such a way that you identify more deeply with the work of God, thinking of yourself as belonging more closely with the people whom God cherishes.

Third, God's loving words to us are an irrevocable promise to give us the hearts and minds necessary to respond to that love. Yet our loving words to God are not so irrevocable, because of our essential inability always to do what we know is good. Our words of loving response, therefore, should always be accompanied by the petition for the grace to carry out what we desire.

YOU MUST LOVE THE LORD

"You must love the Lord your God with all your heart, with all your soul, with all your mind and with all your strength."

1. Contemplate the world of nature around you. Look at the trees, the flowers, the stars above, the planet beneath your feet. None of it had to be, but there it is, radiant and wonderful. Forget the names of things. Look at your surroundings with an artist's eye, wishing you could capture its splendor in paint or stone but knowing your every attempt could not match the glory of the singular, astonishing thing there before you.

Everything in nature speaks. Each thing in itself as well as the entire cosmos is a word, a message, a voice. It tells us, "Pay attention! I am giving myself to you!" It is God's voice, giving humanity a splendid environment, a home, and a message of love. In a mysterious but real way the eternal, unseen God speaks a visible, tangible, and audible word of love for us.

You too are God's word of love to the people around you who can hear it. If you relish this truth, you will want to act on it. Make a covenant with God. Write out an offering you would like to make of yourself.

2. Contemplate the world of history, whose flow you are a part of. Remember the past with a storyteller's affection, wishing you could tell it all but knowing your every story reveals only a glimpse of the great, dark mystery of the emergence and demise of generation after generation.

Then call to mind how God's Word entered human history to give it meaning and direction. Think of how God's Word grew from covenants and laws, through messages to prophets, to the good news of Christ Jesus, who is God's perfect and irrevocable Word.

God has been working throughout history, caring for us, leading us, protecting us. In Jesus we first heard the news that we are reconciled with God and soon realized that Jesus is God's personal entry into our history, teaching, healing, gathering, with the very highest human cost to himself. We learned how intensely God desires to work for us and in us where we are.

By your own words you too give meaning to your historical situation. God has no other voices to speak with except voices like yours. Speak to God about how you want to give your word to others.

3. Consider how God is alive in human hearts. As the very Spirit of the Father and of Christ, God labors incessantly around and within us:

God hovers over creation lovingly, bringing order into chaos. "Now the earth was a formless void, there was darkness over the deep, and God's Spirit hovered over the water" (Gn 1:2). "Like an eagle watching its nest hovering over its young, the Lord spreads out his wings to hold his people" (Dt 32:11).

God makes us like Jesus. We are turned into the likeness of Christ by God who is Spirit. "We, with our faces unveiled, reflecting like mirrors the brightness of the Lord, grow brighter and brighter as we are turned into the image that we reflect. This is the work of the Lord who is Spirit" (2 Cor 3:18).

God welcomes the Word in us. God worked in Mary, Elizabeth, John the Baptist, and Simeon to recognize and welcome the Christ of the Lord. "The Good News came to you not only as words, but as power and as the Holy Spirit and as utter conviction" (1 Thes 1:5).

God in agony cries out in us for freedom. "From the beginning until now, the entire creation has been groaning in one great act of giving birth; and not only creation but all of us who possess the first-fruits of the Spirit, we too groan inwardly as we wait for our bodies to be set free" (Rom 8:23). "God sent the Spirit of his Son into our hearts: the Spirit that cries, 'Abba, Father!'" (Gal 4:6; Rom 8:15).

God heals divisions by working in people spiritually. "There is one Body, one Spirit" (Eph 4:3–4). "Receive the Holy Spirit. Whose sins you forgive, they are forgiven" (Jn 20:22).

God works in all people, drawing them to Christ. "Jewish believers . . . were all astonished that the gift of the Holy Spirit should be poured out on the pagans too" (Acts 10:45).

God's presence in our hearts brings the opposite of self-indulgence. "What the Spirit brings is very different: love, joy, peace, patience, kindness, goodness, trustfulness, gentleness and self-control. . . . Since the Spirit is our life, let us be directed by the Spirit" (Gal 5:22–26).

Then consider that the best way to return love for God is to cooperate with God who labors within you.

4. As a member of Christ's Body, and as inspired by God within, pray the following prayer:

> King God, I am but one voice in your family.
>
> But I praise you today for our minds, for our hearts, and especially for our selves, called from nothing to unending friendship with you.
>
> May we hold your name holy.
>
> May your Kingdom come, and come quickly.
>
> Let us not forget one another but remember and forgive.
>
> Let us turn to you for our daily bread.
>
> Draw us with your grace and your love lest we succumb to temptation.
>
> And may every dawn and every dusk find us grateful as we remember your faithfulness.

Compose your own prayer in a similar vein.

YOU MUST LOVE YOUR NEIGHBOR

*"You must love your neighbor
as yourself."*

1. Read the parable of the Good Samaritan (Lk 10:29–37).
Consider that Jesus created this parable out of his knowledge of the Father and of human nature. Enter into the
consciousness of Jesus, seeing how fittingly this parable represents the love of God the Father. See how in each of us
there is a priest and a Levite who switch to the side of the
road where no one suffers. And there is also a Samaritan in
us, often a rejected side of us, that is moved with compassion and tenderly cares for the victims of the world. Talk to
the Samaritan within you.

2. Sit somewhere where many people gather or pass by.
Watch each person and consider how each one is a veteran
of an interior battle between grace and sin. See how they
are burdened down by false values of society and yet how
love still glows in their hearts. See the scars of that struggle. See in them your own struggles. Let your love and compassion flow out to them.

3. Imagine all of history as a single flow of people, generation after generation, each generation leaving a mixed leg-
acy of the good and the senseless for those who come after.
Think of how the dead live on in the memories, the stories,
the style, and the values of the living. Think about how each
person alive today will enter the cavern of death, joining his
or her ancestors to await the Coming of the Lord. In this
perspective think of how important each moment of life is
and how precious deep human contact really is.

4. Think of how dear someone you love is to you. How most of what you do, you do as a common enterprise, even when he or she is absent. Let yourself realize that not only is your friend a gift but your love is a gift also. God as Spirit recognizes eternal worth in him or her. Be happy to cooperate with that love.

5. Think of how dear you are to someone else. Realize your lovableness, not on any evidence but on the word of the one who loves you. Let yourself realize it not as a matter of self-importance but as an instance of the loving connection God desires between all people, as the work of God's Spirit delighting over you. Consider very realistically how you treat yourself.

6. Pray something like the following prayer:

I believe, my God, that you are absolutely real.

I repudiate my eyes, which report not seeing you;
I repudiate my ears, which say they never heard your voice;
I repudiate my nose and mouth, which prefer sweeter delights;
I repudiate my hands, which feel they were never clasped in yours;
I repudiate my body, which whines for sleep and comfort.

I stand firm in the truth.

I will lean against my culture's frenzied rush past people toward things.
I trust in your great love in me for others.

And I beg you to choose these eyes to catch your searching eye,
these ears to hear your gentle voice,
these two hands to lift up your broken body,
and this body of mine to comfort your aching heart.

Compose a prayer of your own like this one.

Examination of
Consciousness

The first principle for examining your consciousness is never to do it as if you were alone. God dwells and labors in you as a Spirit of Love for you. If you find yourself looking at your failings as a preparation to come to the Lord, then stop. Return to God's presence, a presence in which you think of God as "you" rather than "he" or "she." It is the presence of the prodigal son to his father.

Be particularly ready to express gratitude for what went on in the day. After all, everything good is God's work. God longs to rejoice in the good of others, and God longs to do good through you. The very desire to give thanks will cast a light on even the "good" things you said or did and, at times, reveal a selfish core in them.

Another principle is to recall the true context of your life. The Reign of God grows wherever we follow the voice of love that speaks in our consciousness. Love liberates our consciousness to regard the good of others, to face reality, to be creative in making the world into the community of praise, justice, and peace that God desires and to be watchful for the hand of God in human affairs.

The Reign of God pales wherever we refuse to obey the inner voice of love and instead follow more self-destructive voices. Generally speaking, these self-destructive voices surround themselves with secrecy, suppression, or rationalization, so that they are difficult to notice, even while they lead us to harm ourselves and others.

By failing to pay attention to our inner voices, we ignore uneasy feelings, we neglect to formulate pertinent questions that bother us. By default we miss many opportunities for extending the Reign of God where we live.

A third principle for examining your consciousness, therefore, is this: notice what bothers you. It may be your feelings or your intellect, but you can recognize a concern long before you can formulate it. These concerns may prove valuable to the Reign of God. In particular, if there is any area of your life that you intend to look at but never get around to examining, you have an important clue that you are following a destructive voice but protecting its identity from yourself.

There are four areas in particular that tend to escape our notice: neurosis, class consciousness, story line, and sins of omission.

NEUROSIS

Have you experienced any anxieties, fears, or angers out of proportion to your situation? Are they underreactions or overreactions? Are your dreams telling you anything significant? Are you keeping some action a secret? Are you doing anything compulsively or repeatedly? Are you thinking anything compulsively or repeatedly?

These kinds of eccentricities are to be expected when we are facing some crisis or major decision. They are signs that something we value very much is at stake. Usually it is not too difficult to discover what that value is once we really want to see it. Professional psychological help may be necessary if the behaviors are extreme and no insights are forthcoming about their motives.

Until we understand the neurotic behavior, then, we do not know enough about the movements we experience to evaluate them. We need to understand both what our feelings are and what they are directed toward before we can ask about the value of following where they lead. From a spiritual director's point of view, psychological understanding comes before pastoral counseling and discernment of the Spirit. Similarly, from an ethical point of view, neurotic behaviors are reactive motions not responsible choices. Although they divert our thinking processes and exhaust our energies, they are not yet choices for either sin or grace.

CLASS CONSCIOUSNESS

Class consciousness escapes our notice when we are relatively comfortable. Yet many of our rights may be denied, even in our blissful ignorance.

The key to class awareness is the question of access. Look at the areas of closed access in your life: Are there people you cannot approach? Buildings you feel threatened in? Material resources that are legally available but forbidden by some custom? Church or government institutions that claim to represent you but seem too powerful and remote for you to have any say? Letters you could never send?

Class isolation is closely tied to occupation, sex, race, age, health, titles, clothes, and formal education. Yet in God's Reign there is no Jew or Greek, no slave or free, no male or female. While there is often little you can do to break down the barriers erected by economic concerns, even the smallest step across such barriers is a statement of your belief in the Kingdom of God.

In any case, you can at least break down the barriers that exist in your own mind about other people. Are there people who cannot approach you? Places where you will not welcome others? Material resources you reserve only for certain people? Letters you have not answered? Have you identified yourself with the privileges of a certain class?

STORY LINE

What pride do you take in yourself? What shame do you carry around on your shoulders? What story would you spontaneously tell about yourself today? Is there a different story that may be more true? What story do others tell about you? What story of yourself do you tend to tell others, whether in word or simply by your actions? What stories do you tell yourself about someone close to you?

We have an amazing facility for justifying either a high or a low self-image. We can all give evidence for the stories we narrate to ourselves. The same experience can be data for many different stories.

Once you do recognize a false story at work in your life, reject it. As long as you remain alive your true story is unfinished. It is not yet a tragedy or a romance, not yet a failure or a success.

It takes the eye of love to recognize the story closest to the actual truth. In truth, everyone's story has the same initial plot: the paschal struggle between loving trust in God and fearful trust only in oneself. As long as you live this is your unfinished story. Bring this tale to the light of the cross.

SINS OF OMISSION

Essentially, every sin is a sin of omission because it is first a failure to follow the dictates of reason and conscience and only afterward a destructive act. For those in love with God the number of failures to follow the heart's impulses seems to multiply. We can easily justify these inner refusals because there are no laws against *not* doing something. But that rationalization succeeds only as long as we ignore being in love.

Many moral failures stem from ignorance, weakness, or habit. These are not fully free acts. Yet, in the perspective of a Reign of God in which we are drawn to overcome ignorance, weakness, and destructive habits, we do have a free choice to do something about them. Our sin lies in knowing this and doing nothing.

The most common omission is the failure to reach out to one's neighbor—the sin of the Levite and the priest in the Good Samaritan story. We tell ourselves that we have big business in Jericho and pass by some needy person whom we deem insignificant. Upon examination we often discover that the Spirit did indeed move us to stop going about our business and to pay attention to someone we came upon unexpectedly.

The usual rationale with which we defend ourselves is "I can't do everything!" Indeed, it may not be God's work to drop one kind act in favor of another. This is why it is important to examine one's consciousness. The key question is not "Should I have done X?" (which presumes a merely moral horizon) but rather "Did you move me to do X?" (which presumes a fully religious horizon).

Spiritual Exercises
for Healing[1]

Are These Exercises for me?

These five exercises are meant to help you face something
that hurt you in the past, particularly something that still
hurts.

Usually there is an important person in your life, someone you cared for, who seemed to turn on you. Someone you
trusted who betrayed you. Maybe that person has no idea
that you still bear the scars. Maybe that person has died or
has moved far out of your life. But if you still feel a sting in
the heart whenever you think of him or her, these exercises
may help.

Perhaps you have not been hurt so much by a person
as by an institution—the church, for example, or the school
you went to when you were young, or some company you
worked for that gave you no recognition. You can use these
exercises to bring that wound to Christ too. Just substitute
"church" or "school," or whatever for "persons."

Maybe you think that the hurts in your life are too trivial to dredge up now. But give it a few moments' thought.
You may be embarrassed that you still feel pain over something long past and incidental. But if you do feel the pain,
the incident represents something of deep value to you. And
that value is still in question, even today. You are suffering
an emotional tension, and you have been suffering it for a
long time. Whenever similar situations arise today, you feel

that tension acutely, and it tangles up how you respond to people today. It may be worth your while to bring that old ambivalence to Christ for healing.

What Might These Exercises Accomplish?

You will not be healed of everything that hurts in your life. The hurt that you bring to these exercises will still "hurt" afterward. You may not be healed of anything by simply going through the five exercises once. You will probably not have any resolutions about how to behave from then on. You may not be able to pray more regularly or more easily.

But what these exercises may accomplish is to bring Christ's light and comfort into one painful area of your life. The hope is that even though that area may always hurt, you will be able to face the pain with Christ. Perhaps the habit of facing difficulties with Christ may influence other areas of your life. But now the aim is simply to let Christ come into one significant area with his healing touch.

How Do I Do These Exercises?

The best way is to set aside several days. Five or six, if you can, but two days may be enough. The exercises depend a lot on imagination and feeling and very little on analysis of your compulsions and phobias. (Haven't you done enough of that?) So it's important to be affectively present to your pain for at least several days.

It is also very important to "get the feelings out." I recommend two ways to do this. One is to go through the exercises with someone else. Not that you unload your feelings on the director. Quite the contrary; you share your feelings with Christ. But it's valuable to talk with another human being in the flesh.

The second way to "get the feelings out" is to keep a dialog journal. This is not a journal of your "reflections"; these may be valuable at another time, but not now. In this journal you write out conversations you have with Jesus. At times everything you write will be your own questions and cries. But they should always refer to Jesus as "you," not "he." At other times Jesus may answer you. You are not making up what you think Jesus might say. You really write out words that come as a response to your questions. For example:

YOU: Lord Jesus, I feel as though I've been all alone with this hurt for ten years.

JESUS: No, not alone. I have been here all along.

YOU: But I haven't felt your presence.

JESUS: But I have been here with you.

YOU: If that's true, then why did you put up with all my selfishness and resentments all these years?

JESUS: I'm not going to force you to change.

YOU: Yes, but a little nudge now and then might have helped!

JESUS: Oh, I have been nudging you quite a bit.

YOU: Tell me where!

If you have never done this kind of prayer before, you might find it strange at first. But it is surprisingly easy to tell when the words of Jesus are coming naturally and when you are making them up. When you find yourself making up the dialog, stop. Usually the dialogs last between ten and twenty exchanges, but they can go on longer.

Finally, the first exercise should be done first, and the last exercise last. But the middle three can be done in any order you please, depending on where you are emotionally.

If recalling the hurt makes you feel angry, the second exercise would be good. It brings you before the person who hurt you. If you find yourself clinging to some compromise or "deal" you have made with yourself on account of the hurt, the third exercise will be helpful. And if you primarily feel hard on yourself and depressed at the prospect of facing this pain, the fourth exercise is the one to make. You may repeat any of these three whenever it is appropriate.

1. FACING THE HURT WITH CHRIST

The purpose of this exercise is to get past any denial about the hurt that you have protected yourself with, to let the whole truth come back to memory.

Start with a prayer asking God to be with you during this time. There is no need to spend a long time here, trying to feel God's presence. It will be an act of trust just to ask for this help and then begin to look at your life.

List all the times you have been hurt or at least the major kinds of hurt that you still carry with you today.

Choose one particular time and place that you remember clearly. Choose an experience that is representative of many other times of hurt in your life. Recall every detail of the event that you can—what time of year, what the place was like, how old the people involved were, what time of day. Let the memory replay itself from beginning to end.

What was the very worst part of it? How did you feel as it was happening? If you could change the past, how would you like the same scene to have a perfect ending?

Now let Christ enter that scene, but visible to you alone. Turn to him as if you were now experiencing the scene. Speak your own mind to him. Let this talking with Christ be your "prayer"—whatever comes.

"Freeze" one moment and begin a dialog with Christ, writing down what you say and what he says. Don't be afraid to let your negative feelings come out with Christ, for example, anger, frustration, self-hatred, the feeling that you want to quit, that it's no use, and so on.

End at a natural stopping point. Finish with Psalm 103 or Psalm 86.

2. FACING THE PERSON WHO HURT YOU

The purpose of this exercise is to surface any angry feelings you have toward the person who hurt you.

Reconstruct in your imagination the person who hurt you. Recall the details, his or her face, the words, the actions. Feel the original pain.

Tell Christ how you feel toward this person. Tell Christ what you wish you had said to this person, had you really felt free at the time. Don't be afraid to let feelings of anger come forth.

You may find feelings of love and pity for this person too—at the very same time as the anger. This is a cause of deep frustration. But speak to Christ about those feelings too.

Imagine Christ responding to this person on your behalf. See what he says to this person; watch how Christ deals with them. What does he do? What does he say? (Allow him to be angry too if that's where your imagination takes you.) Turn to Christ yourself and let him know what you're feeling. What does Christ do and say to you? Let the scene unfold in your imagination.

If it seems fitting, write out a dialog between you and Christ. Write out what you feel, as exactly and forcefully as you can. Talk with Christ about any questions whatsoever that you have about the person who hurt you.

End at a natural stopping point. Finish with Psalm 139 ("Lord you search me and know me; You know when I sit and when I stand").

3. FACING YOUR COMPROMISES

The purpose of this exercise is to look at the adjustments you have made in order to live with the hurt.

Reenter the scene. Even though you have done this before, recall to mind all the details. Try to remember parts that slipped your mind previously. Try to see behind even the behavior that you could justify or understand—perhaps you are protecting the person in your mind.

Again, let Christ enter the scene. Now is the time to speak out any "deals" that you have made in your heart. They sound like this: "I will———as long as———." Or like this: "If she would only———, then I would———."

Look at how you behave toward this person to this day, and you will see that you operate out of these secret deals you made with yourself. You probably act toward other people who remind you of this person in the same guarded way. You are trying to protect yourself. You are trying to be "fair." This is completely legitimate and natural. But at least admit to exactly what these deals are.

Tell Christ about them. Write them out as far as you can. What changes would you expect in the person if you are expected to be a better person? What "promises" have you made to yourself or to God about this? What is it you are trying to "buy" by your behavior?

Write these things out in dialog with Christ. Be very honest and humble about it. Let Christ answer you. Write out his words. See the look on his face as you tell him your deals. Ask him for guidance. Insist on it. Pursue it with him.

Let the exercise end at a natural stopping point. Read Lk 22:41–44 ("Father, if you will, take this cup of suffering from me").

4. FACING YOURSELF

The purpose of this exercise is to bring to light the ways in which you blame yourself for being hurt.

Reenter the scene. Recall all the details, but particularly how you felt about your own loss of dignity. Recall any recurring feelings of low self-worth that probably stemmed from that experience. Imagine yourself as the "trash" you felt like, the stick someone just threw away, or the ugly creature people laughed at. Let that symbol of your depression come forth in your imagination.

Let Christ enter the scene. You feel so "wrong" yourself that you want to hide. You don't want him to see you like this. But let him find you.

Tell him why you hide. Tell him the many ways in which you still mask over how low and bad you often feel. List the subtle ways you use to make people think you are not wounded.

Tell Christ how you feel that you have failed. Tell him how you have really destroyed something precious in yourself. Name that precious thing.

Tell Christ how you feel you are separated from him, from God, from goodness. Tell him how unlike good people you feel. Tell him what you wished you had done in the situation.

Let Christ talk to you. Ask him when he felt exactly as you do. Recall that scene from the Gospel. Ask him what he did with those feelings. Let Christ be tender and kind to you. Let him tell you how far he would go for your sake. Ask him.

Absorb Christ's forgiveness and love. Let it come into your heart. Don't be afraid if you think you will have to pay a price for becoming a friend of Christ. Or if you are afraid it will cost you something, tell him what you are afraid of. If you don't know why you fear his love, ask him directly and demand an answer.

Ask Christ how he wants you to behave. Ask him about specific things, whether this or that is what he wants from you right now. He may say that he does not expect any external change, but usually he does want you to receive something interiorly.

End at a natural stopping point. Pray Psalm 32.

5. FACING THE FUTURE

The purpose of this exercise is to go on in life not forgetting the hurt but without letting the hurt destroy you any longer.

Begin by reading Lk 24:36–49. It's the story of Jesus appearing to his friends after his death and resurrection. He explains to them why he had to suffer. He shows them his wounds in his hands and feet. But he comes bringing great peace and assurance.

Enter that scene with Jesus and his friends. You are one of his friends. He wants to be with you; he wants to bring you his enduring peace. You have been wounded, and you still carry a hurt with you. But Jesus has been wounded too; his wounds are still there. Both of you still bear the scars. Ask Jesus how to accept the fact that your wounds, like his, will always be part of your life now, even for eternity.

Look at Jesus' wounds. See in them evidence of a great love. See how God worked through the sufferings of Jesus to rob death of its sting. Look at your own wounds. See in them the mysterious way God works to bring good out of evil. Your wounds are now evidence of something very good. Name that one very good thing about your wounds. Entrust them to God.

This is not a time to make resolutions. Nor should you concentrate on how you will relate to the person or persons who may have hurt you. But you should resolve to accept the basic change of attitude about what hurt you in the past. Decide what you ought to do when the old hurt starts to get power over you and your life again. Ask Jesus for help in getting rid of the leftover resentments and the self-protecting habits you have built around your wounds.

End at a natural stopping point. Pray Psalm 116, a psalm of a person saved from death.

Prayer of Remembering[1]

Many retreatants today come with memories distorted by their own sin or by having been the victims of someone else's sin. It may be important to put these into the fuller perspective of both the good and the bad, done both by me and to me. Here are ten exercises. These may be done in as little as two days, but they can be lengthened if needed.

1. The Good Done to Me:

Parents, brothers and sisters, friends.
Earliest memory? Grade school? High school?
What stands out most this year?
End: ask what role God played.

2. The Good I Have Done to Others:
(not just objective worth—how much time
you gave and how hard you worked—
but internal worth, how much love you
put into it)

Earliest memory? Grade school? High school?
This year.
End: ask what role God played.

Meditative Reading:

3. Jer 29:4–14. I know the plans I have in mind for you, plans for peace, not disaster, reserving a future full of hope for you. When you seek me you shall find me. (In this and the following two texts ask for a deep knowledge of *how* God loves and cares for you.)

4. Lk 12:22–32. Do not worry about your life, what you are to eat, nor about your body and how to clothe it. Look at the ravens, look at the flowers, there is no need to be anxious, little flock.

5. Is 43:1–7. Do not be afraid, for I have redeemed you; you are mine. You are precious in my eyes and I love you. Do not be afraid for I am with you. (In general, instead of contemplating on this fifth meditation, you may repeat a previous one if it seems to beckon you.)

6. The Harm Done to Me:

Both deliberate and indeliberate.
Go over your life history again.

7. The Harm I've Done to Others:

Both deliberate and indeliberate.
Go over your life history.

Meditative Reading:

8. Genesis 2–3. (The sin of Adam and Eve. In this and in the following two texts, reflect on what the author thinks the essence of sin is; compare it to your own spontaneous notion.)

9. 2 Samuel 11–12. (The sin of David)

10. Hosea 1–3. (The sin of Hosea)

Praying the Psalms

The Psalms are considered to be the prayer of God's people. They are essentially a common prayer, even when recited by an individual. It is important, therefore, to realize that you pray them in the place of others who, because of their situation, cannot pray them at this time.

Here is a division of the Psalms according to themes:

Procession/Enthronement: 24b, 47, 68, 93, 97, 98, 99, 132, 149

These psalms all refer not to an earthly king but to the awaited "Day of the Lord" when God would establish a reign of justice and peace, a reign in which all would know the Lord. These can express our hope for the coming of the *Reign of God* on earth that Jesus preached.

Royal: 2, 20, 21, 45, 72, 101, 110, 144

These refer to the presently reigning king in Israel. It may be sung directly to the *person Christ* as King.

Pilgrim: 15, 24a, 50, 78, 81, 84, 87, 91, 95, 100, 121, 122, 133, 134

Good either for *walking* with Jesus as he goes to Jerusalem in pilgrimage or for *longing* to see the church as Bride or Body of Christ.

Praise: 8, 19, 29, 33, 104, 105, 111, 113, 114, 117, 135, 136, 145, 146, 147, 148, 150

These refer to the marvels of God or to some mighty acts of deliverance of ancestors. Good for *general praise* of God.

Thanksgiving: Private: 9, 18, 22b, 23, 30, 32, 34, 40a, 41, 63, 66b, 92, 103, 107, 116, 118, 138. *Communal:* 46, 48, 65, 66a, 67, 76, 124, 129

These always refer to *specific* recent acts of *deliverance.* When praying these, begin by recalling the time and place where the Lord stepped into your life and snatched you from evil.

Wisdom (the just person and the sinner): 1, 10, 11, 12, 14, 37, 49, 52, 53, 73, 75, 94, 112, 119, 125, 127, 128

Like the petition psalms, but more *reflection* on the problem of how God can let Israel *suffer* so, as if God could forget the Covenant. Good for praying for the church when it seems under duress.

Petition: Private: 3, 5, 6, 7, 13, 17, 22a, 25, 26, 27, 28, 31, 35, 36, 38, 39, 40b, 42, 43, 51, 54, 55, 56, 57, 59, 61, 64, 69, 70, 71, 86, 88, 102, 108a, 109, 129, 139, 140, 141, 142, 143. *Communal:* 44, 60, 74, 77, 79, 80, 83, 85, 89, 90, 106, 108b, 115, 123, 126, 137. *Against unjust judges:* 58, 82

Often a cry to be delivered from an *enemy*—enemies of the psalmist, people who hate God, or people who gloat over others' misfortune. Very good for desolation when assailed by "the ancient Enemy." Also some about general suffering or *affliction*. Good for either praying for oneself or praying these words with Jesus suffering, or with any people you know of who are suffering.

Trust: 4, 16, 62, 131

Like psalms of petition but more *confidence* is expressed in God.

A Prayer to
Christ Our Model

by Pedro Arrupe, S.J.[1]

Lord, I have discovered that the ideal of *our* way of acting is *your* way of acting. For this reason I fix my eyes on you; the eyes of faith see your face as you appear in the Gospel.

Lord, you have told us, "I have given you an example to follow." I would like to be able to proclaim, through the faith and wisdom that you give me, what I have heard, what I have seen with my eyes, what I have contemplated and touched with my hands concerning the Word of Life.

Above all, give me that *sensus Christi* St. Paul speaks about: that I may feel with your feelings, with the sentiments of your heart, which basically are love for your Father and love for people. No one has shown more charity than you, giving your life for your friends with that self-emptying St. Paul speaks about. And I would like to imitate you not only in your feelings but also in everyday life, acting, as far as possible, as you did.

Teach me your way of relating to disciples, to sinners, to children, to Pharisees, Pilates and Herods; also to John the Baptist before his birth and afterward in the Jordan. Teach me how you deal with your disciples, especially the most intimate: with Peter, with John, with the traitor Judas. How delicately you treat them on Lake Tiberius, even preparing breakfast for them! How you washed their feet!

May I learn from you and from your ways, as St. Ignatius did: how to eat and drink; how to attend banquets; how to act when hungry or thirsty, when tired from the ministry, when in need of rest or sleep.

Teach me how to be compassionate to the suffering, to the poor, the blind, the lame, and the lepers. Show me how you revealed your deepest emotions, as when you shed tears, or when you felt sorrow and anguish to the point of blood. Above all, I want to learn how you supported the extreme pain of the cross, including the abandonment by your Father.

Your humanity flows out from the Gospel, which shows you as noble, amiable, exemplary and sublime, with a perfect harmony between your life and your doctrine. Even your enemies said, "Master, we know that you teach the way of God in truth and have no regard for personages." The Gospel shows you as hard on yourself in privations and wearying work, but for others full of kindness, with a consuming longing to serve.

You were hard on those in bad faith, but your goodness drew the multitudes. The sick and infirm felt instinctively that you would have pity on them. You so electrified the crowds that they forgot to eat. With a knowledge of everyday life you could offer parables that everyone understood, parables both vigorous and esthetic. Your friendship was for everyone, but you manifested a special love for some, like John, and a special friendship for others, like Lazarus, Martha and Mary. Show me how you expressed joy at festive gatherings, at Cana, for example.

You were in constant contact with your Father in prayer, and your formal prayer, often lasting all night, was certainly a source of the luminous transcendence noticed by your contemporaries. Your presence instilled respect, consternation, trembling, admiration, and sometimes even profound fear from various people.

Teach me your way of looking at people: as you glanced at Peter after his denial, as you penetrated the heart of the rich young man and the hearts of your disciples.

I would like to meet you as you really are, since your

image changes those with whom you come into contact. Remember John the Baptist's first meeting with you? And the centurion's feeling of unworthiness? And the amazement of all those who saw miracles and other wonders? How you impressed your disciples, the rabble in the Garden of Olives, Pilate and his wife and the centurion at the foot of the cross!

The same Peter who was vividly impressed by the miraculous catch of fish also felt vividly the tremendous distance between himself, a sinner, and you. He and the other Apostles were overcome with fear.

I would like to hear and be impressed by your manner of speaking, listening, for example, to your discourse in the synagogue in Capernaum or the Sermon on the Mount where your audience felt you "taught as one who has authority" and not as the Scribes.

The authority of the Spirit of God was evident in the words of grace that came from your mouth. No one doubted that the superhuman majesty came from a close bond between you and the Father. We have to learn from you the secret of such a close bond or union with God: in the more trivial, everyday actions, with that total dedication to loving the Father and all humanity, the perfect self-emptying at the service of others, aware of the delicate humanity that makes us feel close to you and of that divine majesty that makes us feel so distant from such grandeur.

Give me that grace, that *sensus Christi,* your very heartbeat, that I may live all of my life, interiorly and exteriorly, proceeding and discerning with your spirit, exactly as you did during your mortal life.

Teach us your way so that it becomes our way today, so that we may come closer to the great ideal of St. Ignatius: to be companions of Jesus, collaborators in the work of redemption, each one of us another Christ.

I beg Mary, your Most Holy Mother who contributed so much to your formation and way of acting, to help me and all sons of the Society to become her sons, just like you, born of her and living with her all the days of your life.

PART III

Spiritual Guidelines

Revelation

It will be very helpful if we spell out some of the basic truths about God that Christians have learned from experience. At times these truths can bring tears of joy to the eyes and wonderful visions of reality to the imagination. They also serve in times of desolation as rock-solid truths to stand on.

Who is Jesus Christ? He is the perfect Word of God. All of creation and all peoples in history are also God's "word," but they find their meaning and perfection in him. "All things were created through him and for him" (see Col 1:15–20). He is the perfect model of humanity. Through his Resurrection, Jesus lives, still fully human, still at work in history. As God's perfect Word, Jesus Christ is the irrevocable gift of God's own self to humankind; he is the one you have been seeking in all your religious desires.

Who is the Spirit? God's Spirit really has been given as a gift of love within you; you experience God as Infinite Spirit in every act of love. You experience God's gifts as spirit in your heart whenever you experience a rush of faith, of hope, or of charity. This is the Spirit of the Father. The Holy Spirit is the "Sacred Heart" of Jesus. It is the love between them that floods over into love for us. So too our love for God overflows into love for others.

Who is the Father? The Father is the one who gives the Word in history and the Spirit in hearts. These two gifts are self-gifts, revelations of God as essentially a Word-Speaking and a Word-Welcoming Love. There is no experience of Jesus

Christ or of the Spirit that is not also an experience of the single God who is Father, Son, and Spirit.

Who are we? We are a single human race, about five million years old, brothers and sisters sharing common ancestors, living out a single history. From the beginning, as the Spirit of God hovered over the original chaos and the Word of God proclaimed, "Let there be light," we have been God's people, God's desire. God knows all of us, not by knowing each of us but by knowing the community we are born into and become part of. In the fullness of time, Christ Jesus named our solidarity as the "Reign of God," a Reign of praise, love, justice, and reconciliation.

Who are you? You are called from nothing to live forever in solidarity with your brothers and sisters under God. Nothing in your life will be lost in the eternal order of things. By Christian baptism you share in Mary's Motherhood. Like her, you are made worthy by the power of the Spirit to bear the eternal Word on earth today. You share in her astonishment, joy, perplexity, and pain. However, it is also true that you have refused to be led by God, but, despite your shame, are forgiven and called to be a walking witness to God's mercy.

What is the gospel? The gospel is not a book. Nor is it merely a written or spoken message. It is rather an event of hearing God's word being spoken to one personally. There is no good news where the person does not welcome what is heard.

Making a Decision

THREE KINDS OF DISCIPLESHIP

Before deliberating about the choice you face, it may help you to experience your own deepest love for God—and to notice any halfheartedness—by considering the following three kinds of discipleship of Christ.

1. The first kind of disciple has repented of a life of sin and is intent upon avoiding all major sins again. He or she is dedicated to obeying the laws and norms of the church.

2. The second kind of disciple has also repented of sins, but particularly the sins of omission that are seldom prohibited by any rule. Moreover, he or she is ready to accept either good times or bad from God.

3. The third kind of disciple surpasses the first two. This disciple intensely desires to imitate Christ's obedience to the Spirit at every step in life. When, in God's providence, life weighs heavily on others, he or she would rather be with them in suffering than apart from them in comfort. Thus did the Eternal Word and Infinite Spirit choose to be with us.

Think about these different kinds of discipleship throughout the day. Be attentive to any fears or desires you experience about them. Seriously beg the Spirit to give you an authentic and pervasive desire to be called to the third kind.

THREE TYPES OF DELIBERATION

Here is a parable of three couples who have just won a million dollars. But they each feel some uneasiness about what they should do with the money. They would very much like to get rid of the attachment they feel toward the money because it clouds their vision of how to love God.

1. The first couple discusses at length how they can best serve God and neighbor with the money. But their discussion never ends. They die with the money in the bank.

2. The second couple wants to get rid of the pull they feel to spend the money chiefly on themselves, but they want to lose the nagging attachment without actually losing the money.

3. The third couple wants to get rid of the pull to spend the money chiefly on themselves. But they want to do it with a freedom toward keeping or giving away the money. Their main desire is that God's Spirit inspire their choice. Meanwhile, they act as though every attachment to the money had been broken. They make strenuous efforts not to want the money or anything else unless they are moved by God's love.

As you reflect on these three typical ways we make decisions, if you feel a repugnance about the third, it will be very helpful to ask God for the grace of being attracted to the liberation this last way brings. Like the needy friend in the parable, pound on the door, even if it seems too late at night to bother God (Lk 11:5–8).

DIRECTIVES

Here are some suggestions designed to help you make a strategic decision about how you will live your life. For some it means a major decision about marriage or profession. For others it may mean a confirmation of a decision already made. For still others it means a reformation of attitude within a state of life. Often it means a choice of one ministry over another, a choice to pursue or change a relationship, or a choice about where to live.

Courage, Not Deliberation

Before weighing options before you, consider seriously whether or not you already know where God is leading you. Perhaps like Jonah or Jeremiah, you know very well what God is calling you to but have little desire for it. You may know very well that you need help to overcome an addiction, or that you need to take a job with heavy responsibilities, or that you should relinquish your position of power over others. Be careful, in other words, not to engage in some impressive spiritual enterprise instead of obeying the simple voice in you that sees the truth.

In such a case, what you need is courage, not an involved weighing of options. But courage is a gift, not a permanent possession. As you continue to contemplate the life of Christ, therefore, beg him for the courage to do what you wish you could do. Beg God in your heart to drive out your fears and give you the inner assurance that all shall be well, that you will never be abandoned by God. Beg God for the gift of hope, to transform timid and errant desire into confident expectation.

Mixed Motives

There are many interior motives that move a person to choose this or that way of living. And even barring the impulses of pride, there is often a welter of secondary good intentions that blend indistinctly with more fundamental religious motives.

For example, most of us choose something because we feel it will make us happy. Or we may simply want to help others somehow. Some aspire to become persons of heroic virtues because they admire someone very virtuous. But we must admit that we can also be moved by a desire to please our parents or a close friend. We may try to live up to the expectations of others and even of ourselves. We can be moved by a need for security, for warm companionship, or simply for a good self-image. Some of these motives may be more exalted than others, but none of them is sufficient to dispose us to be moved by God.

Yet the presence of mixed motives does not prevent us from being consciously moved by God's love for the world. Even when other motives or advantages accompany a certain option, God may be caring for your situation through you.

The point is to direct your thoughts and feelings toward loving God with all your heart, all your soul, all your mind, and all your strength, and toward loving your neighbor as yourself. Think of this not as a general purpose of your life but rather as the specific motivation of the choice before you. Every good decision ought to keep this simple intention uppermost in consciousness.

If your decision is motived by a desire to love God and to serve God by loving others, no matter what other considerations move you, it will help greatly to learn for yourself that this is indeed your *chief* motive. Then you can thank God for giving you the desire. You can find consolation in the fact that you are fulfilling God's own hope in creating you. When the going gets tough in life, you can much more consciously remember this fundamental love that moved you in the first place.

If, however, you do not know clearly whether you are moved chiefly by this love for God and neighbor, it will be helpful to bring your decision before the Lord again, begging to be given the desire to be moved in your decision solely by this love.

Testing Options

There are several ways to test the options before you.

In the first way, take care to notice whether you experience consolation or desolation when you bring your choice to Jesus in the contemplations. That is, do you feel "centered" in the Lord, or are you "in a mood"? This is particularly true when you feel unsure whether your felt desires are also God's call.

Now, the dynamics of consolation and desolation can be quite subtle—mainly because the evil spirits often give consolation to good persons. So it is very important here to rely on a spiritual mentor or a friend who knows and loves you well. The remarks in "Dynamics of Spirit" (pp. 161–69.) will be especially helpful here.

A second way to test your options is to discuss with others what social and cultural pressures may be preventing you from even experiencing certain desires. These pressures too are very subtle. Many of them come from well-meaning religious officials themselves. Many come from self-images that you have made your own, without examining how they may have restricted your field of vision and action. Call to mind your own vision of the dialectic of desires that underlie the unfolding of history. Call to mind the counter-story of the paschal mystery. Some of the remarks in "Dynamics of Story" (pp. 170–75.) may be of help here.

A third way is to use some of the following exercises. These are a set of techniques designed to help you be as objective as possible about yourself before God.

1. List the pros and cons as you see them. Find advantages and disadvantages for each option.

2. Consider what you would advise someone in your situation. Imagine that this person had an intense love for Christ and an intense desire to bring about the Kingdom with Christ.

3. Spell out the long-range hopes you have for the outcome of a given option. Imagine them in as much detail as you can. Then ask yourself, Is this the Reign of God?

4. Imagine that you are on your deathbed years from now. What decision will you wish to have made then?

5. Imagine that you have died, and that you now come into the presence of the God who made you and whom you have loved from the days of your youth. Imagine your parents and friends as well as all the victims of sin you have ever known there as well. What decision will fill you with the most joy then?

6. Think especially about what your choice will mean for the personal relationships in your life. Compare the important people in your life to Christ. How are they different, how the same? How do they figure in your choice? "Sculpt" your relationships to friends and Christ by imagining where they stand or sit in a room with you. Or imagine that you are on a journey with Christ. Do they walk with you? Behind you? Ahead of you? Are you leaving them behind, or have they chosen to take another road, which may or may not be with Christ also?

The Gift of God's Desire

As you deliberate, be aware that you are not anticipating an insight into the most *cogent* thing for you to do. Nor are you awaiting some mystical *message* from God saying "Do X, not Y." The decision process is simply to beg for a *desire,* springing from love for God, about known alternatives.

Freedom can feel like a terrible burden once we realize that there are no instructions in the mind of God that we must blindly follow. God may seem harshly mute when we ask for a revelation of the divine will. Yet in all truth, God wants to share with us the divine compassion by calling us to choose whatever we want, provided we are motivated by that divine compassion. Jesus himself buckled under the absolute freedom the Father gave him; we can turn to him for companionship in the teeth of a difficult choice.

Beg God to move within you, giving you desire in such a way that it motivates your choice and endures as you live out your choice, no matter what practical difficulties you may encounter.

This desire that you beg for is not simply a desire to *do something*. It is also a desire to become a disciple of Christ in a very specific manner by exercising spiritual authority. This means you are also choosing to be joined to Christ more deeply than ever before. The object of the desire you beg for is simultaneously an action and a self-in-relation. This, after all, is what God desires—not to get mere work out of you, as if you were a hired servant, but to bless you with a new and shared life in the Spirit and the Son, because you are a friend.

As a result, it often happens that your deliberation ends at the point where you say, "I cannot *not* do this." You realize that your own relationship to God is the object of a desire you did not invent but received from the Lord. This is quite different from the adolescent desire to become a somebody, to take on a role in which your relationships gain you admiration and respect. It is a yearning for an integrity dependent on God's Word and Spirit, and deeply and lovingly immersed in the flow of history.

Be Realistic

Throughout this time of deliberation, be as realistic as you can about what is going on inside of you. Be honest about what movements are actually happening in you; don't flinch before the truth of your soul. Beg God to keep you honest about what is happening to your heart. Admit into your consciousness any desires you do have, no matter how embarrassing, because only in facing the truth will you ever be fully alive with the life of God. To fake some desire you wish you had is the beginning of a life built on a wish.

Also, be realistic about what your options actually involve. In every Yes to something you think is good, there is a No to something else—usually another good—which you may feel even more capable of carrying out. In every choice there is a price to pay. You will lose many benefits from options you are leaving. Likewise, you will take on many difficulties connected to the option you choose.

Whether you've already made a decision or not, think ahead: What might block your living out your choice? Trust that God will dissolve that block. Are their any blocks that God wants you to remove *now?* What loss would bring you the most grief? Bring that to Christ, who suffered the loss of everything.

Closure

Be aware that many firm choices prove to be provisional by the vicissitudes of history. Entrust that uncertainty to God, who will be a lamp unto your feet as you walk.

While it is very important to make some decision, be prepared for a "wait and see" outcome. If, in all honesty, you cannot decide, and you know the consequences of not deciding right now, accept this period of waiting in faith as the Lord's will for you now. You are simply choosing, for the love of God, to postpone a final decision.

After several days bring your decision to a close by offering it to God with much diligent prayer, begging that God receive your decision and give you a spirit of inner peace and joy about it. Be grateful for how God has led you to this day. The easier gratitude comes, the more assurance you will have that your choice was prompted by God's own Spirit.

Dynamics of Spirit

These are some guidelines for understanding and dealing with the different events we experience in consciousness.

PART ONE: SPIRITUAL CONSOLATIONS AND DESOLATIONS

1. The imagination and the emotions normally reinforce a person's stance in life, while reasoning and calculation tend to upset it.

2. For example, in people leading a generally self-centered life, their imagination and emotions tend to draw them even further from God. Delights and pleasures fill their memories and hopes. Their thoughts, however, tend to sting their consciousness. So they avoid serious analysis of the long-term consequences of their actions, either for themselves or others.

3. In people leading a generally virtuous life, their imagination and emotions tend to draw them ever closer to God. They joyfully remember good deeds and courageously hope for the best for all concerned. Where they become confused or anxious, it is usually on account of fallacious thinking about what that best might actually be.

4. It is very important to learn, through experience, the difference between *spiritual consolation* and *spiritual desolation*. It is not enough to memorize a definition. Learning the difference is a matter of each person paying attention to his or her own unique, inner experiences and growing accustomed to which ones to trust and which not to. The following descriptions can help us begin to learn about our spiritual dynamics.

5. *Spiritual consolation* includes a range of different experiences. At its peak it is an experience of love for God so direct that everything on earth, including intimate friends and relatives, is loved and appreciated as gifts of God. More ordinarily, spiritual consolation includes the acts of appreciation, of compassion, of kindness, and of hope that usually flow from being in love.

Spiritual consolation is not the same as feeling happy; it can include feeling grief over genuine tragedy, whether our own or others'. It is an experience of feeling centered, at peace within, full of confidence in God. Finally, spiritual consolation is any inner experience or state that enables us to make balanced judgments about reality and wise assessments of the value of persons, words, and deeds.

6. *Spiritual desolation* is the opposite. At its core it is the experience of loving neither God nor neighbor but rather acting out of fear or compulsion. We are "in a mood." We feel dark inside, troubled, anxious, restless, lazy, sad. Or we may feel giddy, scatterbrained, skittish, frivolous, silly. We feel out of touch with our center, separated from God, and alone.

Spiritual desolation is not the same as feeling sad; it can include feeling excited or satisfied, but without any connection to heartfelt love beyond oneself. In any case, it becomes difficult to appreciate people and things around us or to be kind or to have hope in the future. Our thoughts spin wildly but without giving us any help. Finally, spiritual desolation is any inner experience or state that prevents us from seeing reality in its fullest context and from making balanced value judgments.

7. Generally speaking, the reliable realizations, feelings, and proposals that occur to good people have the quality of water penetrating a damp sponge. They begin almost without notice, quickly and softly filling consciousness and easily directing attention to what is true and worthwhile. In contrast, the unreliable inner movements have the quality of water falling on a stone. They are violent, noisy, and disturbing. In people going from bad to worse, however, the effects are just the opposite, with the draw toward inauthenticity feeling natural and gentle while the tug toward authenticity feeling harsh and nagging.

8. Art, architecture, and especially music can evoke either spiritual consolation or spiritual desolation or the tension between them. They can perform this function even when we do not realize it.

9. When we experience spiritual consolation, it is wise to remember that this consolation is a gift, that we cannot create it for ourselves, and that without it we are unable to do much of any worth. In particular, we should recall the times when we knew very well what we ought to do but could not bring ourselves to do it. We can recall how much we needed the gift of courage from God at that point. It also helps at this time to consider how we will act later, when spiritual desolation comes.

10. In a time of spiritual desolation, we should not make any decision but stay with the decision made when we were more at peace.

11. Great courage is required to stand up against the tug toward self-centeredness. If we lose courage and let go of the reins on our hearts, the tug can plunge us into behaviors that we ordinarily are deeply ashamed of. By contrast, if we do something entirely opposite to what that pull suggests, the pull soon loses its force.

12. There are many ways to act energetically against spiritual desolation. If sad, do not withdraw from people but rather make contact. If silly, sober up. It helps to pay close attention to the thoughts that badger us and to see through their fallacies. We should also monitor our feelings and not be quick to value what they value. Take greater care than usual in choosing music and a place to dwell. Although it goes against the grain, we should not slacken our prayer but intensify it. We should not indulge ourselves in excessive eating or excessive recreation or excessive work. In a storm, trim the sails.

13. In spiritual desolation, we can always rely on the truth. We can recall the truths that our faith has taught us, namely, that God will never forget us, that God's Spirit still prays and works in us, that the divine Jesus is still human and suffers his compassion for us. We can recall the truth that desolation does not last forever, even though it may seem so. "I have faith, even when I say, 'I am completely crushed'" (Ps 116:10).

14. A clue to the working of self-centeredness in us is the appearance of a secret that we intend to keep. Just as feeling love is no cause for pride, so being tempted is no cause for shame or secrecy. Candor being the enemy of cunning, once we tell someone else our temptations, their grip on us usually relaxes.

15. There are lessons to be learned from spiritual desolation. If the desolation is our own fault, because we have been listless in our love and have ignored God, we discover the high cost of spiritual inattentiveness.

Another lesson is the poignant realization that spiritual consolation is not within our power to create for ourselves and yet it is necessary for living out a life of love. We learn the lessons of humility and gratitude to the Spirit of God.

A third lesson is the discovery of our secret treasures. Particularly when we face a difficult decision, explosions of fear, anger, or anxiety can erupt in us far out of proportion to the issue. This is because we are secretly guarding something very precious, and its life is being threatened by our deliberation. With some reflection we may uncover what we love so much and whether that love is from God.

PART TWO: THE ANGEL OF LIGHT

1. It is high virtue to aim at discovering what is objectively the best rather than merely knowing what we feel strongly about. But even higher and more liberating is the desire to know what God is calling us to.

2. If we are generally going from good to better, we often experience deep happiness and spiritual joy, which God gives to reveal the divine desire and to energize us for effective love. We also experience deep sorrow and spiritual anguish over the sufferings of others. Our main struggle is with deceptive ideas, complex reasoning, and an overly rational approach to evaluating people and making decisions.

3. The knowledge born of love never brings anxiety, discouragement, or fear. So the thoughts that strike us in desolation can never originate in love, even when their content is true and generally praiseworthy. Likewise, the feelings that occur in desolation cannot be trusted to reveal what is worthwhile.

4. However, although we should mistrust all thoughts and feelings that come in spiritual desolation, we cannot necessarily trust the thoughts and feelings we experience in spiritual consolation. This is a very important and yet easily forgotten lesson in the spiritual life. The following rules explain this in more detail.

5. At times the Spirit may without warning flood our hearts with a sense of God in such a way that we have no doubt about the source of the experience. Often we experience an unshakable conviction about something specific. At other times the experience may not answer certain difficulties that have been on our mind, yet we experience an assurance, a love, a deep-seated affirmation that we are filled with God and that we do not walk alone.

6. Other spiritual consolations well up in response to something we have seen or thought that brings light to the soul. While many of these consolations may be reliable enough, some are designedly destructive of the soul. We experience being filled with light, but as we try to act on it we discover that the original inspiration was a door to fear and worry. Like the angel Lucifer, "Bearer of Light," they lead only to darkness.

7. We should pay close attention, therefore, to the entire course of any spiritual consolation we experience. If we put a good idea into effect and discover a trail of anxiety and confusion, this is a good sign that we have been misled. Here, unfortunately, we can tell the devils only by their trails. But although the damage has been done, we can learn from reflection the kind of spiritual consolations in us that need particularly close scrutiny.

8. Even a spiritual consolation that is undoubtedly from God may be followed by thoughts or proposals that are hardly distinguishable from the original experience of love. These too should be subject to close scrutiny.

9. The Spirit blows where the Spirit chooses. Except where duty requires, the Spirit does not necessarily move us to do every good we are able to. The objective worth of a proposal is not enough warrant for our commitment. Even being anxious about the good we cannot do reduces the good we can do.

10. There are times when we want to do something whose merit is not clear, which is charged with neither consolation nor desolation, but which at least is not contrary to the spirit of legitimate authorities. Before putting it into effect, we often experience a hesitation, thinking that perhaps we are motived by self-gain or some other less worthy motive.

We should trust the living God within us. If our idea is consonant with the love of God, or even if it is simply not contrary to the love of God, we should act on our inspiration. No sense stifling the Spirit because of anxieties about our own virtue and an excessive fear of mixed motives.

11. Good people are prone to ignore small inspirations today to think about greater deeds tomorrow.

Dynamics of Story

1. Events are open to many interpretations using the exact same experiences as evidence. For example, there may be four different stories of the same game of bridge. Or I may say I am firm, while my friend may say I am stubborn. Even within myself I may resent some surgery I had and at the same time see it as a grace.

2. If we believe a story that includes ourselves, we not only find evidence for its plausibility but we tend to continue the story by how we conduct our lives. That is, in many cases we believe first and then create the evidence. We accept the role we have been given in someone else's story, and we then behave in that character.

The battered wife, for example, soon believes she deserves abuse and acts in ways that beg punishment. A successful student, unhampered by the fears of failure that preoccupy an unsuccessful student, is all the more likely to learn what is being taught.

3. The usual attempt to be saved is through the story of being rich and famous. Both the famous rich and the anonymous poor believe it.

4. While some stories patently do not fit the facts, several may. We choose among such plausible stories not on the basis of evidence but under the influence of spiritual consolation and spiritual desolation. (See "Dynamics of Spirit," pp. 161–69.)

Thus, a clear sign of a false or incomplete story is that it leaves us feeling alone, stranded, anxious, confused, afraid, resentful, or bitter. The story may be about success as well as about failure; either way we feel sometimes barren, sometimes jumbled.

A true story will always leave us feeling centered, humble, honest, alive, and in touch with the world around us. It may not be a "pleasant" story. It may be a story of our suffering or even of our own sin; but if we meet our negative experiences with integrity, we sense that we are living in the truth of our souls.

5. The strongest refutation of a false story comes from the truths of our faith. We in fact are never alone. God has promised never to leave us stranded. It remains true that we are temples of God within.

6. Some stories arise from our unconscious, while others originate from our society, our culture, our community. Whatever the case, we very often act out the role assigned to us before we notice the stage we are on.

7. False or one-sided stories arising from the unconscious seem to fear being told out loud. Yet we act out a role that is self-destructive anyway. It is practically useless to consult our experience to determine what we are feeling; repression has masked the feeling, making a variety of different feelings emerge as either anger or hurt or anxiety or fear.

Here it is more helpful to watch our external behavior and, like an impartial observer, conjecture what role we may be acting out. Needless to say, when our behavior is too inappropriate and we are at a loss to explain why, we need help from a professional psychologist.

8. False or one-sided stories originating in our community create the opposite problem; they seem to prefer being told out loud. Our station in life becomes a matter of group pride or at least part of an iron tradition. Worse yet, we often feel a spiritual consolation that is not from God. This consolation is analogous to the "angel of light" (p. 167) temptation mentioned in "Dynamics of Spirit." We feel comfortable with a decision; we enjoy our role; we like ourselves where we are.

9. Besides those provided by consolation and desolation, another clue indicating that we have chosen to believe a false story presented to us by our community is the phenomenon of *closed access*. Are there places you cannot go? Are there people you cannot approach? Materials and services you cannot use? Places where you are out of place? In many such cases there are hidden vested interests at work keeping you "in your place."

Or have you closed access to others, putting yourself behind closed doors, whether in a self-imposed punishment of exile or on a pedestal of honor? Does your station or title prevent others from approaching you? While some isolation is necessary in life, it can convey a story about ourselves that limits our freedom.

10. Another clue that we believe a false story is the experience of a strong desire to *be* something—a teacher, a doctor, a husband, a mother, a minister—rather than a strong desire to *do* something.

To imagine enjoying recognition is to invite spiritual consolation full of blinding dazzle. When God draws our souls, we do not imagine ourselves. We do not feel a glow about becoming somebody. Rather, we feel a sense of self-loss, a risk to our reputation, a need to trust God, and a focus on the neighbor.

11. Closed access and becoming a personage combine in the phenomenon of "mystification." Mystification is talking for the sake of maintaining respect rather than for a desire for the truth. Intelligent-sounding words are used in unintelligent ways. Force of personality replaces appeal to the minds and hearts of others. Mystifying talk prohibits any critical access to the story.

12. The false stories originating from our unconscious can do great damage to our spirits. But the false stories originating from our communities are far more lethal because they deafen the entire community to the word of God and reinforce a community's natural self-centeredness. The spiritual capital of the community is depleted. New members find strange expectations imposed on them and encounter taboos against questioning the status quo. Even if a member is a genius at understanding the dynamics of spirit, he or she has an ever-diminishing potential for naming what is wrong in the community.

13. Essentially, there is only one true story—the paschal story that we each live out. The Law of the Cross belongs to everyone's life. Yet the way in which each person lives it out unfolds only gradually. One's concrete story is unfinished before death. Yet in living out the true story every moment is unique and eternally significant.

14. Prophecy is not a matter of predicting the future; it is telling the true story of the present.

To begin to tell a true story to people clinging to a false one requires an atmosphere of genuine love. Reasoning and analysis will not work because the false stories can all point to experience for reasonable validation. But the true story will point to the further experiences of being drawn quietly within by God, of feeling the risk of self-loss, and of genuine care for one's neighbor.

The true story will see the struggle to name what is really going on as a struggle between the love we feel for God and the fear we feel over losing ourselves. In an atmosphere of friendly love, where people can acknowledge their fears, they more easily recognize in a true story their innermost desires and hopes.

Notes

INTRODUCTION

1. Many of the scriptural passages suggested come from various lists circulated among retreat directors. To a large extent, I have relied on passages suggested by David Fleming, *The Spiritual Exercises of St. Ignatius: A Literal Translation and a Contemporary Reading* (St. Louis: Institute of Jesuit Sources, 1978), 154–57, and *Place Me With Your Son: The Spiritual Exercises in Everyday Life* (Georgetown: Georgetown Univ. Press, 1986), 5–16.

SPIRITUAL EXERCISES FOR HEALING

1. Adapted from Matthew and Dennis Linn, *Healing Life's Hurts: Healing Memories Through Five Stages of Forgiveness* (New York: Paulist Press, 1978). The practice of writing dialog prayers with Christ comes indirectly from a technique of dream analysis suggested by Ann Faraday in *The Dream Game* (London: Temple Smith, 1975).

PRAYER OF REMEMBERING

1. Taken from David Hassel, "Prayer of Personal Reminiscence: Sharing One's Memories with Christ," *Review for Religious* 36 (1977): 213–26.

A PRAYER TO CHRIST OUR MODEL

1. Slightly abbreviated and recast. From "Our Way of Proceeding" by Pedro Arrupe, S.J., in Jerome Aixala, ed., *Other Apostolates Today: Selected Letters & Addresses,* Vol. III (St. Louis: Institute of Jesuit Sources, 1981), 350–55.